New Directions for
Higher Education

Martin Kramer
EDITOR-IN-CHIEF

Changing
General Education
Curriculum

James L. Ratcliff
Kent Johnson
Jerry G. Gaff
EDITORS

Number 125 • Spring 2004
Jossey-Bass
San Francisco

CHANGING GENERAL EDUCATION CURRICULUM
James L. Ratcliff, D. Kent Johnson, Jerry G. Gaff (eds.)
New Directions for Higher Education, no. 125
Martin Kramer, Editor-in-Chief

Microfilm copies of issues and articles are available in 16mm and 35mm, as well as microfiche in 105mm, through University Microfilms Inc., 300 North Zeeb Road, Ann Arbor, Michigan 48106-1346.

NEW DIRECTIONS FOR HIGHER EDUCATION (ISSN 0271-0560, electronic ISSN 1536-0741) is part of The Jossey-Bass Higher and Adult Education Series and is published quarterly by Wiley Subscription Services, Inc., a Wiley company, at Jossey-Bass, 989 Market Street, San Francisco, California 94103-1741. Periodicals Postage Paid at San Francisco, California, and at additional mailing offices. POSTMASTER: Send address changes to New Directions for Higher Education, Jossey-Bass, 989 Market Street, San Francisco, California 94103-1741.

New Directions for Higher Education is indexed in Current Index to Journals in Education (ERIC); Higher Education Abstracts.

SUBSCRIPTIONS cost $80 for individuals and $160 for institutions, agencies, and libraries. See ordering information page at end of book.

EDITORIAL CORRESPONDENCE should be sent to the Editor-in-Chief, Martin Kramer, 2807 Shasta Road, Berkeley, California 94708-2011.

Cover photograph © Digital Vision

www.josseybass.com

CONTENTS

EDITORS' NOTES

Bringing about any change in higher education is difficult. Curricular change is particularly challenging. The time-worn adage is that it is more difficult to change a college curriculum than to move a graveyard. And then there is general education. General education gets defined in different ways—philosophically, historically, structurally, or relationally.

General education curriculum is an integral part of the American undergraduate education course of study. Its heritage as a formal academic program began with William Rainey Harper's founding of the Junior College at the University of Chicago and the founding of the General College at the University of Minnesota (Ratcliff, 1997a). Over the years, there have been periodic examinations of how general education has been organized, conducted, and changed. In roughly ten-year intervals, Dressel and De Lisle (1969), Blackburn and others (1976), Toombs, Fairweather, Amey, and Chen (1989), and Gaff (1991) examined general education across American higher education institutions. Since the Gaff (1991) study, however, no national study of general education had been conducted. Here we take a practical, operational view of general education as a formal component of undergraduate education outside of the major, specialization, or discipline all students are required to take (Conrad, 1978; Toombs, Fairweather, Amey, and Chen, 1989).

This volume is about changing the general education curriculum—in big ways through significant reforms and, more frequently, incremental ways—to accomplish purposes better, to connect with students better, and to provide a more engaging and intellectually and emotionally compelling common collegiate experience. The chapters in this volume present the results of a recent national survey on change in general education curriculum; four case studies of institutions that have undertaken change (how they did it, what the constraints were, and most important, what the results were); and concluding discussions on the unfinished agenda of curricular coherence and the nature of change and when and how to bring it about.

General education is that ill-defined portion of the undergraduate curriculum that belongs to nearly everyone and is the sole province of no one. Although it may be the component of associate and baccalaureate degrees with the largest number of student enrollments and the greatest number of faculty members enlisted in its teaching, it frequently lacks its own organization, budget, and dedicated faculty. In a recent reaccreditation report to the Middle State Association of Colleges and Schools, a university (which shall remain mercifully anonymous) stated that although it had general education courses that all students must take, it had no general education program; rather, various departments offered the courses, and their impact on student learning was therefore difficult to assess. If general education is an overt component of a degree program and students are required to complete courses to fulfill that component, then the university has a general education program. Nevertheless, it is often the disciplinary departments that supply the instructional corps of general education, and it is most often those same departments that are fiscally rewarded for their success in servicing this central piece of the academic pie. General education frequently is governed by a revolving cadre of faculty drawn from the various disciplines contributing courses to its requirements. The faculty committee that oversees the general education curriculum, if the institution has one, tends to draw those interested in internal institutional service and those committed to preserving the resources accruing to their departments from the general education program. An associate provost, dean, or director frequently administers a program taught by borrowed faculty who seldom, if ever, convene to discuss the aims, organization, and outcomes of general education. More often, such faculty governance arrangements become the venue for determining which courses are approved to "count" as meeting general education degree requirements, thereby ensuring the offering departments and their faculty fully-enrolled, full-time-equivalent revenue-generating courses. Such subsidies have little to do with the aims, purposes, and assessments of student learning in general education. Thus, general education comes to the institutional planning and budgeting process as a stepchild and an afterthought. If change in higher education is complex and change in curriculum is especially thorny, then change in general education might be thought to be nearly impossible.

In fact, change and innovation in general education is not only possible but also prevalent. Under the auspices of the Association of American Colleges and Universities (AAC&U) and the Center for the Study of Higher Education at Pennsylvania State University, we undertook two surveys in 2000—the GE 2000 survey of directors of general education and the CAO 2000 survey of chief academic officers—of baccalaureate-granting institutions and found a majority to be engaged in general education change and innovation (Ratcliff, Johnson, La Nasa, and Gaff, 2001). Here we report trends and findings from these surveys pertinent to changing the general education curriculum. In addition, we invited case studies of institutions that have planned and implemented general education curricular change. These cases add context and variety to the notion of general education change. What we learned about change and about the unfinished agenda of curricular reform is reported here, as are the cases of four such institutions that undertook their own journey to change general education. In charting what changed, we have come to regard a curriculum as a key representation of knowledge, culture, scholarship, and perspective from which students of various backgrounds, interests, and abilities experience, discover, and gain understanding (Ratcliff 1997b).

In Chapter One, we describe and summarize what we learned about change from a decade of general education reform and revision. The GE 2000 and CAO surveys provide a broad-stroke picture of the activity, the changes, the organization, and the future of general education as we crossed into the new millennium. Like most other portraits, however, these surveys give a snapshot in time. To put this picture into perspective, we compare and contrast with two prior studies. Ten years earlier, Gaff (1991) surveyed chief academic officers, and Toombs, Fairweather, Amey, and Chen (1989) conducted a detailed and comprehensive examination of general education as reported in college catalogues. Taken together, the GE and CAO 2000 survey results and the comparisons with studies a decade earlier provide a picture of how change in general education is accelerating, what has motivated that change, and why. Far from the impossible, general education reform, revision, and redesign is not only possible but is found widely throughout higher education today.

Four case studies of changes in general education at different types of institutions add context to the survey results. The first of our case stories, the development of the general education program at Franklin Pierce College, chronicles a quest to create a distinctive curriculum—one that would differentiate this small New Hampshire liberal arts college from its competitors and one that reflects a commitment to long-term, deliberative planning. The story is one of success in overcoming faculty inertia and budgetary limitations to achieve in 1990–91 a major overhaul of the general education program. The Pierce Plan exemplified some of the major curricular trends found in the GE 2000 survey and best practices in program design found in the literature. It provided interdisciplinary seminars in each of the four years of study, including a first-year seminar, the "Individual and Community," and a capstone senior liberal arts seminar. Sophomore general education courses, such as "The Ancient and Medieval World," integrated history, literature, the visual arts, music, philosophy, and religion into an interdisciplinary framework rather than requiring course work in each of those separate subjects as is found in a conventional distribution general education plan. As Sarah T. Dangelantonio recounts in Chapter Two, this was a curricular revolution followed by a decade of evolutionary fine-tuning. In the process of refining, many of the unique features were improved and embellished, while others fell into disfavor and were threatened with discontinuance. The original curricular overhaul was not informed by data on student learning or formal reviews of the program; it was an imaginative creation of the faculty and academic leaders to articulate the mission and values of the college. The refinements and modifications are now informed by students' assessments and program reviews and stimulated by the standards of the New England Association of Schools and Colleges, of which Franklin Pierce is an institutional member in good standing. Today, program evaluation and student assessments, together with systematic planning, guide the evolution of general education.

The second case, presented by Haig Mardirosian in Chapter Three, examines the general education reforms at American University in Washington, D.C. Here a new general education program began in 1989 following discussion, design, and planning over the preceding two years. Like the Pierce Plan, American University sought to create a distinctive curriculum that fit the international and cosmopolitan character of its students and distinguished it from its competitors. A second and equally important motive was to improve the coherence of the curriculum, convey its value to students, and overcome the sense among students that general education was "a knot of requirements" difficult to navigate. Six objectives for general education were derived from institutional mission and values. Five curricular areas addressed these objectives through the provision of clusters of courses organized by themes, a strategy used in many other institutional reforms of the decade. A ceiling of 150 courses was established for all of general education so that the clusters needed to be created from a constrained (rather than ever increasing) bevy of subjects. The reforms at American University illustrate a problem that general education faces at many institutions: the intersection between the expectations of professional fields on general education and the competition for curricular space between major and general education course work. As at Franklin Pierce, the general education program at American University was the creative work of the faculty and academic dean and originally was not informed by program reviews and student assessment. In 1999, the program was revisited more formally as part of the strategic planning process, the presidential discussions on the future of the university, and the application of revised standards during the reaccreditation visit of the Middle States Association of Schools and Colleges. Thus, again, the tools of evaluation and assessment, the structure of strategic planning, and the influence of regional accreditation conspired to prompt further refinement and reform.

Our third case story, Cascadia Community College, presents a very different situation. Many who have labored at general education reform wish that they could wipe the slate clean and not be bound by departmental politics and the vested interest of faculty members who take offence when it suggested that the course they have taught for countless years will no longer be part of the new general education curriculum. Cascadia is a new community college in Washington State, and its leaders were challenged with creating general education from scratch. Yet as Victoria Richart notes in Chapter Four, Cascadia's initial curriculum was designed within a web of constraints. The college was to share facilities and provide programs that made for easy transition for students to the University of Washington, Bothell. The curriculum needed to address the Direct Transfer Agreement of the Higher Education Coordinating Board and the statewide articulation agreement of the public institutions of higher education, and it had to meet candidacy requirements for accreditation by the Northwest Association of Colleges and Schools. Thus, the educational, social, and political context in which the college undertook its initial curricular design created a gravity toward the conventional and safe—perhaps a distributional plan. However, the campus leadership boldly adopted the principles of a learning organization, derived four broad goals for the educational program from the mission statement, and developed interdisciplinary courses organized as learning communities to enable students to achieve these aims.

At the same time, the same goals concurrently guided faculty development through the Teaching and Learning Academy and employee development through the Employee Learning Institute so that the entire campus community—faculty, administration, staff, and students—worked toward common goals as a learning organization. Each goal in the common core of learning competencies was steered by a learning outcome team comprising faculty, staff, and administration and charged with the fulfillment and refinement of the goal. To ensure the ongoing connection and relevance of the curriculum to business and industry, major employers as well as many of the area institutions receiving Cascadia transfer students served on advisory groups that contributed to the review and evaluation of the programs. Cascadia embedded conventional general education subjects found in the articulation agreement into the learning community course clusters. Cascadia not only illustrates how one college designed general education from scratch using available literature on best practices in undergraduate education but did so imaginatively and without succumbing to the conventional credit distributions expected by articulation agreements.

The final case story comes from Hamline University in St. Paul, Minnesota. If Cascadia is the youngest of general education programs presented here, then Hamline is the oldest. The Hamline Plan, instituted in 1984–85, gives the longest look at change in general education curricula reported in this volume. There was a sense then that the conventional "two-of-everything" distributional curriculum was out of date, was not connected to the mission of the university, and provided no distinctive basis on which applicants might select Hamline over the other colleges and universities in the metropolitan Twin Cities area. As Garvin Davenport relates in Chapter Five, general education before the reform was seen as something for students to "get out of the way for the major." Its purpose was "opaque" and its relation to the major and the professional fields was "uncertain and unexplained."

The Hamline Plan focused on the "practical liberal arts," drawing a connection to the university's many career-oriented and professional majors. It implemented many of the innovations that were to become widely used in reforms of the 1990s: theme-related year-long first-year seminars, writing-intensive courses, and emphases on speaking, computer literacy, diversity, leadership skills, and internships. The courses incorporated and addressed more than one general education area, were team based, and stressed the development of problem-solving skills. Like Franklin Pierce and American University, the realization of the Hamline Plan was followed by what Davenport calls "a second wind of change." As with the initial redesign of general education, this second wind portends the future in general education reform: explaining the pedagogy of interdisciplinarity, exploring the mean of breadth in relation to the study of culture and diversity, reexamining the curricular conventions of time, course, and credit, and using assessment as an informative tool to spotlight what works and highlight agendas for further curricular change.

In developing these case studies, we asked each author to describe certain aspects of the changes at their institution. Rather than simply reiterating goals and requirements, we asked them to describe the forces and factors that led to the particular configurations they adopted; to profile how those changes were communicated to administrators, faculty, and students; and to assess how the changes had fared over time. These stories show how change is not only feasible but also achievable.

In Chapter Six, we take up one of the more elusive characteristics of the curriculum: coherence. In reviewing the data from the GE 2000 and CAO 2000 surveys and the four cases, Kent Johnson and James Ratcliff note that most colleges strive to improve coherence, but most fall short of the mark. They examine why. Tensions are inherent in the general education curriculum and commonly are viewed as barriers to coherence. These tensions often are about what to teach and why, how to organize the curriculum, whether classic or contemporary texts should prevail, and to what extent personal development or communal and civic goals should prevail. There are tensions between general education and the major, the professional fields, and graduate education. Also, general education is the source of debate relative to social relevance and purpose of the undergraduate curriculum and to who gets to decide (the institution, the system, or the legislature) what general education should be provided. Conventional approaches to changing the curriculum emphasize the resolution of such tensions as a first step, usually through consensual decision making in a task force or committee. Johnson and Ratcliff assert that such an approach may inhibit rather than facilitate change and present an alternate view of these tensions as integral to progress toward coherence. The authors offer four criteria for planning for the improvement and evaluation of curricular coherence, describing it as a great unfinished agenda in general education reform. They find that increased curricular coherence improves public understanding of general education and provides new vitality and shared understandings of the program by students and faculty.

The increasing prominence given to changing the general education curriculum in the 1990s was paralleled by the adoption of more rigorous planning, budgeting, and evaluation systems in colleges and universities. This second trend altered the first; how general education curriculum is changed has changed, argues James Ratcliff in the seventh, and concluding, chapter. Changes to general education over the decade clarified goals; limited student course choices; and refocused programs from the introduction to disciplines to interdisciplinary groupings around themes, clusters, and learning communities. In addition, courses on diversity widely became part of most programs. By and large, these changes were not necessarily a result of strategic plans, program reviews, or student assessments, yet increasingly colleges and universities vet general education change within the larger context of mission, strategic planning, and evaluation policies. Ratcliff asserts that the current processes of academic planning and evaluation, now so firmly entrenched, may have limited utility when change is directed to the improvement of quality or coherence in general. The conflicting and sometimes contradictory nature of program quality has practical consequences for curricular change and specific implications for the use of the planning and evaluation paradigm.

The quality of general education is influenced strongly by formal and informal communication. While the university catalogue may put forth lofty goals, faculty advisers may tell students to avoid a course or get it out of the way, redefining its expectations and importance. Communication engenders understanding, conveys the values, and helps define the quality and coherence of the program. Through communication with one another, people articulate multiple and often opposing viewpoints. Thus, discussions of general education become unfinished, ongoing social discourses. Discussions about curricular quality and coherence emerge from tensions endemic to the concepts themselves and therefore are not simply solved. Contradictions and tensions are inherent in general education, such as the prescription or election of courses, disciplinary and interdisciplinary learning, and learning organized by cohorts of students and that arranged by sequence of subjects.

Contradictions, Ratcliff asserts, are the basic drivers of both incremental and transformative change. Concepts derive their meanings from one or more opposing concepts. The idea of the capstone course emerges from the lack of synthesis among disparate courses. The marriage of curriculum concepts with opposing ones fosters the social dynamics of change that may have both-and rather than either-or attributes.

Ratcliff examines certain key question in the change process, such as whether the focus should be on the improvement process itself or a set of desired outcomes and how to regard curricular churning relative to progressive, cumulative change. He finds that change has involved more than merely stating an educational goal around which faculty teach and students learn; it also attends to how that goal is discussed, understood, and redefined by faculty and by students and how that continuous re-envisioning becomes manifest in the program.

No book, particularly an edited book, can come together without the assistance, encouragement, and advice of others. To that end, we thank Carol Geary Schneider, president of the Association of American Colleges and Universities, for her counsel on the design and execution of the GE 2000 survey and for the good offices of AAC&U in carrying it out. Similarly, we thank Steve La Nasa, now of George Mason University, for the design and implementation of the electronic questionnaires used in the GE 2000 and CAO 2000 surveys. Finally, we express our sincere appreciation to Martin Kramer, editor of the New Directions for Higher Education Series, in his patient and selfless insistence that this project be brought forth. However, what has resulted from this project remains our own, and we take responsibility for what we present in the anticipation that it will provide guidance in designing a more engaging, thoughtful, coherent, and effective general education program.

References

Blackburn, R. T., and others. *Changing Practices in Undergraduate Education.* Berkeley, Calif.: Carnegie Council on Policy Studies in Higher Education, 1976.
Conrad, C. F. *The Undergraduate Curriculum: A Guide to Innovation and Reform.* Boulder, Colo.: Westview Press, 1978.
Dressel, P. L., and De Lisle, F. *Undergraduate Curriculum Trends.* Washington, D.C.: American Council on Education, 1969.
Gaff, J. G. *New Life for the College Curriculum: Assessing Achievements and Furthering Progress in the Reform of General Education.* San Francisco: Jossey-Bass, 1991.
Ratcliff, J. L. "Quality and Coherence in General Education." In J. G. Gaff, J. L. Ratcliff, and Associates, *Handbook of the Undergraduate Curriculum.* San Francisco: Jossey-Bass, 1997a.
Ratcliff, J. L. "What Is a Curriculum and What Should It Be?" In J. G. Gaff, J. L. Ratcliff, and Associates (eds.), *Handbook of Undergraduate Curriculum: Innovation and Reform.* San Francisco: Jossey-Bass, 1997b.
Ratcliff, J. L., Johnson, D. K., La Nasa, S. M., and Gaff, G. J. *The Status of General Education in the Year 2000: Summary of a National Survey.* Washington, D.C.: Association of American Colleges and Universities, 2001.
Toombs, W., Fairweather, J. S., Amey, M., and Chen, A. *Open to View: Practice and Purpose in General Education 1988. A Final Report to the Exxon Education Foundation.* University Park: Pennsylvania State University Center for the Study of Higher Education, 1989.

James L. Ratcliff
D. Kent Johnson
Jerry G. Gaff
Editors

JAMES L. RATCLIFF *is president and senior consultant, Performance Associates Postsecondary Consulting, Pueblo West, Colorado.*

D. KENT JOHNSON *is director of assessment services at the Arkansas State University, Jonesboro, Arkansas.*

JERRY G. GAFF *is senior scholar, Association of American Colleges and Universities, Washington, D.C.*

1

From 1990 to 2000, there was widespread change in general education. What do the trends say?

A Decade of Change in General Education

D. Kent Johnson, James L. Ratcliff, Jerry G. Gaff

Those engaged in or contemplating changes in the general education program may find the trends uncovered in the GE 2000 (Ratcliff, Johnson, La Nasa, and Gaff, 1999a; Johnson, 2003) and CAO 2000 surveys (Ratcliff, Johnson, La Nasa, and Gaff, 1999b; Johnson, 2003) interesting and useful. These were complementary cross-sectional surveys in 2000 of 567 baccalaureate-granting institutions that were members of the Association of American Colleges and Universities (AAC&U). The sample was approximately proportional to the number of baccalaureate colleges, master's-degree-awarding colleges and universities, doctoral-granting institutions, and research universities in the United States.

Two complementary questionnaires were devised drawing on the instruments and findings of two prior studies a decade earlier (Gaff, 1991; Toombs, Fairweather, Amey, and Chen, 1989) so as to permit analysis of that which had changed. The first survey was sent to chief academic officers (the CAO 2000 survey) to gather their institutional perceptions. In addition to sharing their own views, the CAOs identified the individual most responsible for administering the general education program at their institution. This person then was contacted and asked to answer more detailed questions regarding the general education program and its policies and practices (the GE 2000 survey). As might be imagined, many CAOs, particularly at smaller institutions, were also the primary administrator of the general education program and completed the GE 2000 survey themselves. After adjusting for undeliverable e-mail, the sample size for the CAO survey was 521 institutions, and we received responses from 278, for a response rate of 54 percent. Two hundred responses were obtained from the GE 2000 survey,

Table 1.1. The Year General Education Was Last Revised

Year Revised	Number of Institutions	Percentage of Institutions
Before 1979	17	6.1
1980–1989	46	16.5
1990-present	206	73.8
Missing responses to question	10	3.6
Total	279	100.0

Sources: Johnson (2003); Ratcliff, Johnson, La Nasa, and Gaff (2001).

which was 69 percent of the CAO responses. Ratcliff, Johnson, La Nasa, and Gaff (2001) presented initial results from the surveys, and Johnson (2003) described fully the methodology and major findings. Here we focus on what they told us about change in general education.

Nearly all (99.6 percent) of the responding CAOs at the 278 baccalaureate-granting institutions said their institution placed a higher priority on general education in 2000 than it did ten years earlier. Over half of these CAOs (53 percent) thought faculty also placed a higher priority on general education in 2000 than a decade earlier. Curiously, though, most were dubious of the effect these new priorities had on students. Only fifty-seven CAOs (21 percent) believed their students placed higher priority on general education than those attending ten years earlier.

Not only was general education a higher priority for academic leaders and faculty; change was in the works. Nearly three-fourths of the CAOs (74 percent) reported their current general education program was most recently revised during the 1990s. Of those instituting change within the 1990s, more than three-fourths (81.0 percent) said their programs had been changed in the past six years (between 1994 and 2000). Slightly more than 16 percent (16.5 percent) had last changed general education in the 1980s, and only 6 percent had last changed their program prior to 1979 (Table 1.1). Most institutions modified their general education programs in either large or modest ways during the decade, and the majority of revision came in the latter half of the decade.

Which Institutions Were Changing Their General Education?

Changes in general education occurred in all types of institutions awarding the bachelor's degree. Common arguments against general education, such as, "Our institution is just too large and complex to change its general education," or "Our college is just too small and lacks the resources necessary to carry out a new general education curriculum," simply were not sustained by the data.

A greater proportion of master's institutions (82 percent) revised their general education programs between 1990 and 2000 than did either baccalaureate (77 percent) or research and doctoral institutions (67

Table 1.2. Year of General Education Revision by Institutional Type

Institutional Class	General Education Last Revised		
	Before 1979	1980–1989	1990-Present
Research and doctoral	6.3% (n = 4)	26.6% (n = 17)	67.2% (n = 43)
Master's	2.1% (n = 2)	15.8% (n = 15)	82.1% (n = 78)
Baccalaureate	10% (n = 10)	12.7% (n = 14)	77.3% (n = 85)

Sources: Johnson (2003); Ratcliff, Johnson, La Nasa, and Gaff (2001).

percent). Master's-degree-granting institutions were most frequently the site of change, and it was not clear from the data as to why this was so. However, more important, changes in general education were occurring in all types of institutions awarding the bachelor's degree (Table 1.2).

In 2000, at What Stage in the Change Process Were Institutions?

Were the colleges and universities surveyed merely talking about change in general education? Had they designed new curricula? Were they in the process of implementing reforms? And were they evaluating the impact of changes on student learning? General education administrators (GEAs) at institutions surveyed answered these and related questions (Table 1.3).

The clear majority of GEAs (80 percent) reported that their general education programs were currently being revised in 2000; only one in five GEAs (19 percent) reported that revisions were not under way. Three overlapping thirds of the respondents are worthy of note. First, a third of the colleges and universities surveyed (32 percent) were discussing changes to their general education programs. Second, a third of the institutions (31 percent) were conducting a formal review of their programs at the time of the study. A third (32 percent) were assessing their general education programs. Also, forty percent of the institutions were implementing changes to general education that year. These responses were nonexclusive of one another; several institutions were engaged in some combination of discussing, reviewing, implementing, and assessing general education. These findings remind us that change is often a messy process; it does not typically move in a straight line from discussion, to design, to implementation, and then to evaluation. The majority of institutions were implementing a recent set of revisions while initiating ongoing discussions of further changes.

Table 1.3. Planning and Implementing Change to General Education

	Planning Change Next Year	Not Planning Change Next Year
Changing program	73 (42.4%)	66 (38.4%)
Not changing program	27 (15.7%)	6 (3.5%)

How Long Does It Take to Change a Curriculum?

A survey is admittedly a single snapshot and therefore an imperfect indicator of change over time. Nevertheless, the GE 2000 survey did provide some clues as to how long colleges were taking to plan and implement their changes. Table 1.3 shows that 43 percent of GEAs indicated that they were revising their curricula in 2000 and that they planned to continue that activity into the next academic year, making it a multiyear initiative. Slightly less than that, 38 percent, were revising their general education program in 2000 but were not contemplating further revisions in the following year. Sixteen percent had not yet begun curriculum revisions but were planning to do so in the next academic year. And only 3.5 percent were neither revising the general education program in 2000 nor contemplating doing so the following year. Over 96 percent of all GEAs were either revising their program or were planning to revise their programs the following year. Clearly, if revision of the general education curriculum is complex and difficult, these institutions and their leaders were not shy in giving priority to, reviewing, and designing formal plans for change.

The CAOs at these institutions saw general education programs to be ever changing and saw such change as largely incremental rather than a one-time comprehensive overhaul event. One noted the curriculum "is dynamic" and requires "constant revision and updating." Another stated that changing general education was a "long process" and that the goal for general education reform at the institution was to create "a more integrated and responsive general education curriculum" that was "more manageable and assessable." Another characterized general education reform as a continuous process, observing, "The last full revision followed an extensive review of undergraduate education. It has changed in small ways several times since and is under ongoing review."

What Qualities Did General Education Programs Possess?

We asked the CAOs to rate several aspects of their programs using a five-point scale ranging from "not at all" to "very much." Most of the general education changes in program characteristics appeared to be mission driven. Sixty percent of the respondents indicated that general education goals were closely related to institutional mission "very much," and nearly 38 percent believed their general education goals followed the institutional mission "quite a lot." Mission, more than student needs and expectations or social issues and context, guided the design of general education.

Within the context of conventional curricular components—goals and objectives, sequence and organization, instruction strategies and delivery, and assessment and evaluation—it is interesting to note where the CAOs believed their general education programs had strengths and weaknesses.

General education goals were clearly stated "very much," according to 36 percent of the CAOs; an additional 36 percent believed that their goals were clearly stated "quite a lot," indicating that some required further work. Less than 17 percent thought that their general education goals were somewhat unclear or not clear at all. Goal clarity apparently was a curricular priority largely achieved in 2000.

Were the general education course requirements clearly linked to the goals? Were there, for example, corresponding goals to the requirement that students complete nine credit hours of social science course work? Or did the curriculum have a clear means for students to develop critical thinking or leadership goals? Slightly more than one-fourth (28 percent) reported that the linkage between goals and course requirements was "very much" the case, and 36 percent stated that most requirements were linked to goals "quite a lot." In harmony with conventional curriculum planning perspectives, most CEOs reported having general education goals that were tied to institutional mission and regarded them as clearly stated. A third of the institutions linked the specific general education course requirements to those goals.

Although coherence is a commonly stated aim of general education, it is difficult to achieve in practice. When asked whether their programs had coherent sequences of courses, the CAOs acknowledged that this was the case "very much" or "quite a lot" in only 38 percent of the cases. Distribution requirements, the most common form of general education, permit student choice, faculty autonomy, and ease of administration. But it is difficult to make linkages across courses developed, taught, and studied separately.

Less effort had been given to assessing what students learned as a result of their general education program. Only 14 percent of the institutions reported that student learning was assessed "very much" in relationship to the general education goals. Another 17 percent said that student learning was assessed "quite a lot," and 30 percent said that such assessment occurred "somewhat." Another one-quarter (24.5 percent) stated "not very much" assessment took place, and a final 15 percent confided that assessment occurred "not at all." Although it has been an expectation of higher education curricula for nearly fifteen years, assessment of the broad goals of general education has been limited. Determining how much and in what areas students have successfully mastered the capacities intended for them in general education has yet to be a guide in choosing what programs to revise and how.

What Practices Were Included in the General Education Curricula?

Drawing on recent literature on curricular change and innovative practices, we asked the CAOs to report the extent to which some of the most frequently mentioned innovations were included in their current general education programs (Table 1.4).

Table 1.4. Prevalent Curricular Innovations

Curricular Innovation	Mean Response	Standard Deviation
Interdisciplinary courses	3.51	1.20
First-year seminars	3.37	1.66
Common learning	3.32	1.24
Advanced courses	3.13	1.50
Honors courses	2.99	1.46
Experiential learning	2.74	1.27
Paired or linked courses	2.64	1.33
Senior thesis	2.42	1.51
Service-learning	2.40	1.27
Internships	2.14	1.30
Independent study	2.09	1.25
Remedial or developmental	1.99	1.30

Sources: Johnson (2003); Ratcliff, Johnson, La Nasa, and Gaff (2001).

The general education programs of these institutions were more likely to have incorporated interdisciplinary courses, first-year seminars, common learning experiences, advanced courses, and honors courses. They less frequently included experiential learning, paired or linked courses, a senior thesis, service-learning experiences, internships, independent study, or remedial or developmental courses. These findings were consistent with what Gaff (1991) found ten years earlier. Many of the innovations he reported as important curricular trends in 1990 were now integrated in the general education programs. Others, however, remained largely topics for discussion and debate but were not yet widely adopted in the curricula.

Different types of institutions were more inclined than others to adopt particular innovations or practices. Common learning experiences were slightly more likely features of general education programs in baccalaureate and master's institutions than in research universities and doctoral institutions. Research universities and doctoral institutions were more likely to provide honors courses in general education than were master's or baccalaureate institutions.

Did the Changes in General Education Alter the Credit Distribution in the B.A. or B.S. Degree?

In 1991, Gaff reported an average forty-nine credit hours were allotted to general education, noting that slightly less than 40 percent of the total hours in a baccalaureate degree were general education courses. Toombs, Fairweather, Amey, and Chen (1989) found that forty-seven semester credits (38 percent) and sixty-five quarter credits (35 percent) were allotted to general education for the B.A. degree (Table 1.5). In the GE 2000 survey, general education composed 38 percent of the credits for the B.A. and 38 percent of credits for the B.S. degrees. The mean number of semester hours

Table 1.5. Credit Hours Required for B.A. and B.S. Degrees and General Education

	Mean Hours Required, B.A. Degree	General Education as % of B.A. Degree	Mean Hours Required, B.S. Degree	General Education as % of B.S. Degree	Mean Hours General Education
Hours	125.46	37.59%	125.83	37.48%	47.16
SD	17.43		19.38		13.02

Sources: Johnson (2003); Ratcliff, Johnson, La Nasa, and Gaff (2001).

for general education requirements was 47.[1] Thus, although most colleges and universities were changing their general education curricula, they did so without altering significantly the amount of total credits required or the proportion of credits attributed to general education in baccalaureate degrees.

We should note, however, that there was large variation about these means, indicating that the number of credits in general education varied greatly from institution to institution, as did its proportional credit role to the total baccalaureate degree requirements. Unlike Toombs, Fairweather, Amey, and Chen (1989), we did not find the required number of general education hours to vary by institutional type. Also, the number of general education hours required of the B.A. and B.S. degrees was nearly identical, and this finding did not vary by institutional type or control (public versus private).

What Role Did Program Review Play in the Change Process?

Program evaluation can be an important means to identifying discrepancies between desired and actual performance or capacities, the discrepancies then becoming the directions for change (Gates and others, 2002). To what extent, then, was change guided by formal program reviews? When institutions conducted such a review, they focused on the clarity of its goals more frequently than any other element or component of the program. This was consistent with the priorities that the CAOs and GEAs gave to goal clarity. Other program characteristics regularly subject to review were the extent to which the curriculum contained diversity perspectives, provided a synthesis of learning experiences, afforded students smooth transition to collegiate studies, and developed specific skills, competencies, or proficiencies. These foci of program review paralleled those found a decade earlier by Gaff (1991) and Toombs, Fairweather, Amey, and Chen (1989). As Table 1.6 illustrates, program review in general education remained confined to certain conventional elements of the curriculum.

Table 1.6. General Education Areas Reviewed

Targets of Formal General Education Program Review	Number of Institutions Reviewing	Percentage of Institutions Reviewing
Clear goals	107	60.5%
Diverse perspectives	89	50.3
Synthesizing learning experiences	88	49.7
Making transition to school	76	42.9
Skills in field	72	40.7
Coherence	69	39.0
Overcoming deficiencies	59	33.3
Working with others	57	32.2
Integrating in-class and out-of-class learning	52	29.4
Students shaping their learning	42	23.7

Sources: Johnson (2003); Ratcliff, Johnson, La Nasa, and Gaff (2001).

It stands to reason that if an element of general education is deemed important, it should be included as part of the formal review criteria for the program. This is what we found. A chi-square analysis showed that when a priority was placed on setting clear goals, the GEA reported including goal clarity in the program review process ($p < .001$). Also, GEAs who gave priority to coherent sequences of courses were likely to review the extent to which such sequences helped achieve goals ($p < .001$). However, although coherence was given as a principal reason for revisions and reforms, most institutions did not specifically review their programs for coherence. Fewer than half (43 percent) reported reviewing courses designed to assist students' transition to college. More than half (58 percent) reported reviewing first-year seminars, a major vehicle for facilitating the transition to collegiate studies. Half reviewed the provision for teaching diversity issues in general education, and of those institutions, 43 percent required specific diversity courses in their general education programs. With the exception of program coherence, our survey results gave a consistent picture of the alignment of general education priorities with program review criteria.

Comments from the CAOs indicated that some institutions began the reform process with a program review—for example, "It had been over ten years since we last reviewed the curriculum and the statistical (and actual) quality of the entering students had significantly changed." Still others started from a general sense of the faculty's desire for change. One CAO, for example, reported that general education reform at his institution was "based on faculty wishes to provide a coherent and distinctive general education program for students reflective of both the institutional mission and liberal arts tradition."

Thus, while general education was most frequently subject to periodic program review, it was not clear the extent to which these reviews were used as a basis for improving the general education programs.

What Role Did Assessment of Student Learning Play in Reform Efforts?

Along with program review, assessment of student learning commonly is thought to provide valuable information on what is working and what is not in curricular programs and to be an important guidepost to changing the curricula (Paloma and Banta, 1999). A decade earlier, Gaff (1991) found that assessment of general education was "increasingly common, both to identify problems that call for change and to determine the extent to which a new curriculum is effective" (p. 58). The study by Toombs, Fairweather, Amey, and Chen (1989) of catalogue descriptions of general education did not find comprehensive assessments of student learning in general education programs reported. It should be noted that publication of a practice in a college catalogue often follows rather than precedes the implementation of the practice, such as the addition of new courses or experimental activities. Toombs and his colleagues found that where student assessments were listed in the catalogue as required, they were used to determine specific skills through proficiency testing and to place students in an initial set of courses.

Had things changed over the decade? Had assessment of student learning become an important part of the change process? We compared those institutions making changes in their programs with those that were not relative to their reported use of assessments of student learning outcomes in general education.

Table 1.7 shows that only 15 percent of institutions had assessed student learning outcomes at the time they were implementing changes in general education, and 25 percent were making curricular changes without the guidance of student assessment information. Another 18 percent were assessing student outcomes but not implementing any changes to their general education program. Clearly, having an overall assessment of student learning as a component of general education was no guarantee or indicator that such information would be used in the change process. After nearly twenty-five years of the student assessment movement in higher education and the urgings and the discourse on the subjects by national associations, such as the American Association for Higher Education's Assessment Forum, and by the requirements of state coordinating and governing bodies, through the guidelines of the regional accrediting associations, and by the stipulations of various federal programs affecting higher education, it was disconcerting to see so little implementation and apparent use of comprehensive assessments of student learning outcomes in changing the general education curriculum. Yet the survey facts provided a sharp contrast to the rhetoric regarding student assessment. Only 32 percent of the CAOs and GEAs reported assessing student learning in their general education programs. Thus, less than one-third of institutions evaluated whether students were accomplishing the goals of their general education programs.

Table 1.7. Assessment and General Education Change

	Making Changes in General Education		Not Making Changes in General Education	
	Number	Percent	Number	Percent
Assessing student outcomes	23	15.3%	27	18.0%
Not assessing student outcomes	38	25.3	62	41.3

Sources: Johnson (2003); Ratcliff, Johnson, La Nasa, and Gaff (2001).

Although the comprehensive assessment of student learning within general education programs was present in less than one-third of institutions, there were assessments of specific general education content or skill areas in considerably more institutions (see Table 1.8). Component-specific assessments were far more prevalent in general education than were comprehensive assessments of student learning. These findings reinforced the view that disciplinary departments remain highly influential over the conduct of general education, including the assessment of student learning.

Over 75 percent of institutions have goals relative to the traditional content divisions of liberal learning—natural sciences, social sciences, and humanities—and over half of those with stated goals assess student learning in the related general education component (Table 1.8). While over 80 percent have goals in reading or writing, or both, and mathematics, over two-thirds of these institutions assess student learning in these components. With the exception of collaborative work, lifelong learning, global studies, and cultural diversity, over half of institutions having goals assessed student learning on those goals. Thus, when one examines specific components of general education, the profile of assessment of student learning outcomes becomes more positive.

As was the case with program review, however, just because an institution assessed student learning outcomes relative to a general education goal did not mean that the assessment information was used in the change process. Evaluations of general education, whether they are program reviews or assessments of student learning, continue to play an uncertain role in reform efforts.

What Reforms Most Frequently Were Implemented?

We found most curricular changes undertaken over the decade to be modifications to existing general education programs rather than complete revisions or remaking of the courses of study. Although the CAOs indicated that general education had become a higher priority at their institutions, their changes to the curriculum did not alter credit requirements significantly. General education had about the same proportion of credits of the bachelor's degree in 2000 as in 1989. However, as we will describe in the next section,

Table 1.8. Student Assessment in General Education Components

General Education Component	Institutions with a Stated Goal for the Component		Percentage with a Stated Goal for Component That Assesses That Goal
	Number	Percent	Percent
Content areas			
Natural sciences	150	87.7%	57.3%
Social sciences	145	81.9	56.6
Math/quantitative	140	79.1	61.4
Humanities	131	74.0	54.9
Fine arts	124	70.0	54.8
History	105	59.3	61.9
Literature	101	57.1	65.3
Philosophy, ethics	99	55.9	58.5
Foreign languages	83	46.9	63.8
Physical sciences	71	40.0	56.3
Life sciences	68	38.4	57.4
Religion	66	37.3	59.1
Cognitive skill areas			
Reading/writing	156	88.1	77.6
Critical thinking	119	67.2	64.7
Speaking/listening	98	55.4	68.4
Computing	92	51.9	64.1
Other components			
Cultural diversity	113	63.8	44.2
Global studies	92	51.9	46.7
Interdisciplinary	70	39.5	52.8
Lifelong learning	57	32.2	40.3
Collaboration/teamwork	36	20.3	38.9
Leadership	19	10.7	63.2

Sources: Johnson (2003); Ratcliff, Johnson, La Nasa, and Gaff (2001).

the general education requirements became more prescriptive, reducing student choice. By and large, these institutions did not turn to a strictly prescribed core curriculum in making their changes. Rather, they relied on themes to unify required sequences and clusters of interdisciplinary course work to achieve their ends. This is a major shift from the 1980s, when student choice was a primary trait of general education curricula (Toombs, Fairweather, Amey, and Chen, 1989).

What Courses Were Added or Dropped?

Toombs, Fairweather, Amey, and Chen (1989) at Pennsylvania State University examined general education requirements in college catalogues. We compared these decade-old data with those from the GE 2000 survey to determine what courses had been added or dropped from general education requirements and what trends these changes might signify (Table 1.9).

Table 1.9. Course Requirements in General Education

General Education Component	Percentage of Institutions Requiring Courses in Component		Modal Number of Course Credits Required in Component	
	Catalogue Study, 1989	GE 2000	Catalogue Study, 1989	GE 2000
Interdisciplinary	19.4%	63.9%	3	3
Humanities	96.7	91.7	12 (6)*	3
Fine arts	53.3	86.8	3	3
Math-quantitative	64.8	92.1	3	3
Social science	96.1	93.9	6 (12)*	6
Natural science	93.7	89.8	6	6
Foreign language	33.5	59.0	6 (12)*	6
Physical education	52.9	67.9	2	2
Values	28.4	59.6	6	6
Computer	11.0	47.5	3	3
Other	32.2		6	
Collaborative work		15.8		3
Critical thinking		48.0		3
Cultural studies		66.2		3
Global studies		58.3		3
History		88.2		3
Leadership		2.9		3
Lifelong learning		9.3		3
Life science		59.1		3
Literature		83.3		3
Philosophy		73.1		3

*Denotes bimodal distribution.

Sources: Johnson (2003); Ratcliff, Johnson, La Nasa, and Gaff (2001); Toombs, Fairweather, Amey, and Chen (1989).

From 1989 to 2000, general education course requirements changed in several respects. Most noticeably, the number of required components to general education had grown. Course work was now required in areas such as critical thinking, cultural studies, global studies, history, life sciences, and literature. Courses in foreign languages, computer literacy, and values education were added. However, these additional requirements came about while the proportion of general education credits required in the baccalaureate degree remained fairly constant. By 2000, student election of course work in general education had declined significantly as a greater proportion of institutions had specific requirements in all subject areas examined. The notable exceptions were in the general requirements in the humanities, social sciences, and natural sciences.[2] The GE 2000 survey contained several specific disciplinary or skill areas that would be part of the broad humanities, natural science, and social science categories of Toombs, Fairweather, Amey, and Chen (1989).

Among those general education areas common to both studies, the largest increases were in interdisciplinary studies, mathematics and quantitative skills, values, and computer literacy. Also in 2000, institutions prioritized students' understanding of other cultures (66 percent of institutions) and the complexities of global issues (58 percent of institutions). These increased course work requirements confirmed the continuation of trends first noted by Toombs, Fairweather, Amey, and Chen (1989) and Gaff (1991).

How Did Institutions Organize the Changes in Their Programs?

Were most general education programs still distributional, or was the trend in 2000 toward a core curriculum? Several respondents to the GE 2000 survey indicated that they found it difficult to report exact credit requirements to specific content and cognitive skill categories. These respondents noted that their general education programs had shifted from traditional content and skill distribution categories (for example, three credits in history, six in writing) to required themes or clusters of course work where required content and skills were integrated into interdisciplinary clusters and sequences and unified by themes. For instance, one GEA stated that the conventional categories of the GE 2000 survey did not "represent separate phenomena" in their general education program, as several of the skill areas listed on the questionnaire were now "embedded in the Integrative Studies courses" of the general education program. A second GEA commented:

> Our lower-division learning communities create the possibility of interdisciplinary teaching and learning and require thematically linked content courses in either the sciences or the humanities or the social sciences. While we have no requirements specific to global studies, several of the learning communities have global themes. Both collaborative work and leadership are general education program outcomes and the learning communities are meant to incorporate activities and learning adapted to those outcomes.

Yet a third GEA described general education areas as "interdisciplinary areas of understanding that are not tied to disciplines or departments." A fourth described how general education skills were embedded in the program rather than individual courses: "Reading, writing, speaking, information literacy, critical thinking, and creative thinking are required in every general education course." Finally, another GEA observed, "Our choices do not mirror your categories. They include cultures and civilization and studies in aesthetic experience, for example." These comments explain the increases in institutions with interdisciplinary requirements (from 19 percent in 1989 to 64 percent in 2000) as reported in Table 1.9. Campus leaders saw the goal of required themes or clusters of courses to increase coherence and provide greater meaning across the curriculum. Also, these leaders saw curricular themes connecting study across disciplines and permitting the inclusion of innovations such as learning communities, service-learning, reflective essays, and capstones.

Both CAO and GEA respondents claimed that themes were used to make the learning experience coherent, help students bring meaning to their general education program, and provide students the opportunity to make connections between their education and social issues. While the GE 2000 survey did not reveal any clear trend away from distributional elective curricula or toward prescribed core curricula, it did show increased prescription of courses in a greater number of curricular areas and the use of curricular themes and clusters to convey the organization of general education curricula.

Were the Changes in General Education Due to External Pressures?

Over the decade, a number of states and higher education systems implemented policies for student transfer and articulation of credits that may have affected general education. Also, many of these agencies mandated accountability and assessment reporting that may have influenced the general education program as well. Regional and specialized accrediting agencies changed their standards relative to general education (Ratcliff, Lubinescu, and Gaffney, 2001). The standards for the Accrediting Board for Engineering Technology and the Commission of Higher Education of the Middle State Association of Colleges and Schools, for example, strengthened standards with direct implication for general education. Thus, although there are many potential external influences on the curriculum (Garcia and Ratcliff, 1997), our survey examined those we thought most likely to have an impact on general education programs and those that had been examined in prior studies.

Nearly two-thirds of the institutions (63 percent) reported at least one external influence on general education. However, sources of influence varied greatly across institutions, and no single external factor that was identified affected a majority of institutions. Also, while the sources of external influence did not vary according to institutional type, they did vary predictably between public and private institutions. Over eighty percent (83 percent) of public institutions claimed that one or more external factors affected general education. Fewer than half of the private institutions (49 percent) reported one or more external source of influence.

The most frequently cited external influence on general education, regardless of institutional type or control, was the regional accrediting association. Thirty-eight percent of CAOs and 46 percent of GEAs saw the revision of accrediting standards as affecting change in the general education program. As Table 1.10 shows, this influence varied significantly by

Table 1.10. Influence of Accrediting Agencies on Changes in General Education

Regional Accrediting Association	Total Number of Institutional Members in Accrediting Region	Changes in General Education Reported to Be Influenced by Accrediting Agency Standards	
		Number	Percentage
Middle States	73	16	21.9%
New England	28	12	42.9
North Central	84	29	34.5
Northwestern	12	4	33.3
Southern	63	36	57.1
Western	19	9	47.4

Sources: Johnson (2003); Ratcliff, Johnson, La Nasa, and Gaff (2001).

accrediting region. Institutional members of the Southern Association of Colleges and Schools (SACS) most frequently (57 percent) found their general education programs affected by the association's standards. Nearly 50 percent of the reporting members of the Western and New England associations found that the standards of these bodies were relevant to their general education programs. Respondents from other regions less frequently cited their accrediting associations as influential over general education.

Specialized accrediting agencies, highly influential on requirements for majors in professional and career fields, were not seen as particularly influential on general education. One in four GEAs (25 percent) found that the standards of specialized accrediting groups played a significant role in changes to general education. One in four GEAs (24 percent) saw interinstitutional or statewide articulation agreements influencing general education reform. Only 12 percent of GEAs noted that the interventions and legislation of state government influenced changes in their general education programs, while 12 percent saw state coordinating boards influencing the changes in their general education programs. These forms of external influence were felt particularly in public institutions. Nearly four of ten GEAs (39 percent) at public colleges and universities saw their general education programs influenced by statewide agreements on articulation and transfer; only 12 percent of private institutions reported a comparable effect.

Respondent CAOs elaborated on the external influences affecting general education in open-ended portions of the survey. These were the increasing emphasis on student learning outcomes and competencies, the strengthening of specific components of general education, the mandating of course content through articulation agreements, and the easing of general education credit recognition for transfer students.

What Were the Major Reasons for Change?

While there was clearly external influence on the changes in general education during the decade, principally by the regional accrediting associations and particularly among public institutions affected by legislation and statewide coordination, the primary impetus for change came from within the institutions. In analyzing the open-ended commentary of CAOs to the survey, three reasons for reform stood out:

- The general education program was fragmented and had little coherence.
- Changes in the students or faculty required changes in general education.
- The program was outdated.

Analysis showed that 54 percent of the CAOs giving open-ended commentary on their surveys cited achieving greater curricular coherence or reducing curricular fragmentation as the primary reason for reforming the general education program. Nearly half (48 percent) also found the general education program failing to meet student or faculty needs and therefore in need of change. Over one-third (38 percent) described their programs as out of date and therefore deserving of change.

Achieving Greater Coherence. Most CAOs expressed needs to make general education curricula more coherent. Collectively, the respondents did not show a uniform notion of what coherence was or how it was to be achieved. They proposed a variety of paths, including tying general education to the major, to mission or goals, and to a reduction in general education course offerings. Most gave multiple reasons for a lack of coherence. For example, one saw the lack of coherence in general education due to inadequate integration with the major, stating that the "program was modified to integrate it more effectively with programs in the schools and departments."

Many CAOs saw coherence best achieved through a closer linkage of general education purposes with institutional mission. One CAO explained, "Currently we are developing an entirely new general education program because we need to tie general education to mission; the current curriculum is out-of-date and does not address coherency or needs, and it does not have adequate assessment." Other CAOs discussed achieving greater coherence through the reduction of distribution requirements, the movement to a core curriculum, or the tightening of existing core curricula. In 1991, Gaff reported that curricular leaders believed that reducing student options in general education would generate greater coherence. A decade later, many leaders continued to act on that belief, adding greater prescription and reducing student election in general education.

Over the past decade, there has been considerable discourse on fragmentation in the curriculum and the merits of focusing course work on specific skills or competencies to gain coherence. This appeared in some survey commentary on change in general education. One CAO said the recent revision in general education was to "integrate the teaching of competencies across the curriculum." Another noted, "The general education package of courses had grown uncontrollably over the years. There was a lack of coherency of offerings, with awful disconnection of learning and skill-building experiences." Yet another illustrated the problem of fragmentation: "The previous program had become very unwieldy. It was a distributional model with nearly 350 course options. The aims and goals of the program were vague. It had been revised piecemeal over the years." Although there is some question as to whether reducing course offerings increases coherence (Ratcliff, 1997, 2000; Stark and Lattuca, 1997), several institutions changed their general education curriculum for this reason. But as we have seen, only 38 percent of CAOs thought the changes adopted in general education brought about increased coherence.

Meeting Student and Faculty Needs. Changes in general education also came about as a result of perceived faculty or student needs. Faculty needs were often cited by CAOs as a primary reason for change. For example,

> There was a sense of weariness among faculty who had carried the main teaching load in certain parts of the program. In particular there was a sense that it would be refreshing and possibly result in more effective pedagogy if we abandoned several of the common syllabus courses that had characterized our approach for many years in favor of common themes around which individual faculty would structure their own syllabi.

General education also was changed in response to student needs. Frequently, general education was changed to be more responsive to first-year students. Also, programs were changed to meet new goals specifying student learning outcomes and competencies needed for graduation. Some CAO respondents indicated that general education had been modified due to the need to assess student learning.

Student concern about the quality of course work and lack of full-time faculty involvement in general education prompted some reforms. One CAO commented, "The need to redesign our required freshman seminar was prompted by concerns about lack of involvement by full-time faculty across the disciplines and student concerns about variability in quality and confusion about intended purposes of the course."

The skills and abilities that college graduates need provided the focal point for other reform efforts. One CAO noted, "It was time to revise our plan, given the significant changes at the institution and the various post-baccalaureate cultures into which our graduates were moving. We wanted to address development of competencies such as multicultural global issues and technology, and strengthen critical thinking and problem solving, for example."

Many of the changes were incremental in nature, taking the form of an update rather than a wholesale revision. A respondent explained, "Our general education program was revised to update it according to student needs and to add an integrative capstone course."

In an era of tight resources and competition for students, several changes were made to attract and retain students and to respond to the changing demographics of the student population: "Student retention was decreasing. The preparation level of entering students is continuing to be lower than in the previous decade and their attitudes toward education and difficult work are also lower. As a commuter campus, we thought that a greater sense of community was needed."

Updating the Program. Several CAOs described the general education programs as having a "shelf life" and therefore needing periodic changes. One noted, "The old plan had been in effect for ten years and was due for review." Another tied the vitality of the program to broader social change: "Our previous curriculum was over fifteen years old and did not reflect realities of today's life." Still another thought that general education became outdated when it no longer related to the students. The programs had been revised in many cases by adding specific courses in diversity and multiculturalism, computer literacy and the use of technology, and understanding the impact of the increasing internationalization of society. The changes came at the expense, in credit hours, of the broad divisional categories of humanities and arts, social sciences, and sciences found in many of the predecessor distributional plans for general education.

A Decade's Worth of Change

The decade of change in general education was largely incremental and sustained trends noted at the outset of the decade by Toombs, Fairweather, Amey, and Chen (1989) and Gaff (1991). These curricular changes sought coherence using two primary approaches. First, student election of course work was reduced, while prescribed sets and sequences of courses increased. Second, course work was grouped into themes and clusters to better communicate the relationship between the different subjects, skills, and fields of knowledge contained therein. These changes were often associated with tying the general education program closely to institutional mission more than to meeting student needs or social expectations.

External factors seemingly played a relatively modest role in general education change. They swayed public more than private institutions. Regional accrediting agencies were influential over the general education programs of their members. However, the majority of change was brought about internally by the good efforts of faculty and academic leaders on campus.

Academic leaders increasingly saw general education as a dynamic program, needing to adjust and respond to the changing needs and interests of students, society, and the expanding realms of knowledge. The changes over the decade were largely incremental and intended to make general education programs more coherent, to meet needs of students and faculty better, and to update their programs based on societal and institutional changes. These changes were largely structural in nature, including increased prescription of courses, increased attention to issues of diversity and global issues, increased emphasis on interdisciplinary study, and increased use of thematic curricular designs in general education.

In the chapters that follow, these decade-long trends in general education change are further unpacked in the case studies of four institutions. The stories illustrate that general education is tied inevitably to institutional context. Each curriculum differs in educational philosophy or philosophies, students served, programs offered, constituencies served, institutional mission, and other factors. The value of learning from others' experiences in general education reform, then, is one of analogy, allegory, and adaptation rather than adoption of approach and practice.

Notes

1. The Gaff (1991) and Toombs, Fairweather, Amey, and Chen (1989) studies differed in a variety of ways but reported comparable results. Gaff studied institutions that were changing their general education programs, while Toombs, Fairweather, Amey, and Chen studied a randomized sample stratified by institutional type. Gaff surveyed chief academic officers, while Toombs, Fairweather, Amey, and Chen studied college catalogues. Toombs, Fairweather, Amey, and Chen reported the proportion of the baccalaureate credits assigned to general education only for the bachelor of arts degree. The CAO 2000 survey most paralleled that of Gaff in that it surveyed chief academic officers and drew its sample from AAC&U, an association that may attract institutions interested in change in general education.

2. Although the data showed that 3 to 5 percent fewer institutions had specific natural science, social science, and humanities requirements, this finding may be an artifact of differences between the GE 2000 survey and the catalogue study conducted by Toombs, Fairweather, Amey, and Chen (1989).

References

Gaff, J. G. *New Life for the College Curriculum: Assessing Achievements and Furthering Progress in the Reform of General Education.* San Francisco: Jossey-Bass, 1991.

Garcia, M., and Ratcliff, J. L. "Social Forces Impacting the Curriculum." In J. G. Gaff, J. L. Ratcliff, and Associates (eds.), *Handbook of Undergraduate Curriculum: Innovation and Reform.* San Francisco: Jossey-Bass, 1997.

Gates, S. M., and others. *Ensuring Quality and Productivity in Higher Education: An Analysis of Assessment Practices.* San Francisco: Jossey-Bass, 2002.

Johnson, D. K. "General Education 2000—A National Survey: How General Education Changed Between 1989 and 2000." Unpublished doctoral dissertation, Pennsylvania State University, 2003.

Palomba, C. A., and Banta, T. W. *Assessment Essentials: Planning, Implementing, and Improving Assessment in Higher Education.* San Francisco: Jossey-Bass, 1999.

Ratcliff, J. L. "What Is a Curriculum and What Should It Be?" In J. G. Gaff, J. L. Ratcliff, and Associates (eds.), *Handbook of Undergraduate Curriculum: Innovation and Reform.* San Francisco: Jossey-Bass, 1997.

Ratcliff, J. L. "A Model for Understanding Curricular Coherence and Transparency." Paper presented at the Annual EAIR Forum, Freie Universitat Berlin, Germany, Sept. 7, 2000.

Ratcliff, J. L., Johnson, D. K., La Nasa, S., and Gaff, J. G. "GE 2K Survey Instrument." [http://www.ed.psu.edu/cshe/htdocs/research/ge2000/ge2000.html]. 1999a.

Ratcliff, J. L., Johnson, D. K., La Nasa, S., and Gaff, J. G. "CAO 2K Survey Instrument." [http://www.ed.psu.edu/cshe/htdocs/research/ge2000/cao_survey.html]. 1999b.

Ratcliff, J. L., Johnson, D. K., La Nasa, S. M., and Gaff, G. J. *The Status of General Education in the Year 2000: Summary of a National Survey.* Washington, D.C.: Association of American Colleges and Universities, 2001.

Ratcliff, J. L., Lubinescu, E. S., and Gaffney, M. A. (eds.). *How Accreditation Influences Assessment.* New Directions for Higher Education, no. 113. San Francisco: Jossey-Bass, 2001.

Stark, J. S., and Lattuca, L. R. *Shaping the College Curriculum: Academic Plans in Action.* Needham Heights, Mass.: Allyn & Bacon, 1997.

Toombs, W., Fairweather, J. S., Amey, M., and Chen, A. *Open to View: Practice and Purpose in General Education 1988: A Final Report to the Exxon Education Foundation.* University Park: Pennsylvania State University Center for the Study of Higher Education, 1989.

D. KENT JOHNSON is director of assessment services at the Arkansas State University, Jonesboro, Arkansas.

JAMES L. RATCLIFF is president and senior consultant, Performance Associates Postsecondary Consulting, Pueblo West, Colorado.

JERRY G. GAFF is senior scholar, Association of American Colleges and Universities, Washington, D.C.

2

Reform at Franklin Pierce College was first envisioned as a revolution. As the reform progressed, it became a dynamic evolution, responding to changing needs.

The Franklin Pierce Plan

Sarah T. Dangelantonio

The March 19, 1990, minutes from the Curriculum Committee at Franklin Pierce College, note, "After reviewing the history of deliberation, time and effort (the Committee has been at this since late August), the Committee voted that our report to the faculty, at the April meeting, shall be the following: 'Our search into core reform has been non-conclusive, and after consideration, we have chosen to call a moratorium upon the subject.'"

We were not going to talk about core reform because we could not find any common ground. Since we could not agree on what a core curriculum should accomplish, we could not agree on what its basic components were. After eight months of discussions during the 1989–1990 term, only two written responses to the dean's proposed curricular changes had been submitted. In an undated memo to the faculty, the chair of the Curriculum Committee summarized the situation in the following way: "There is apparently little enthusiasm among the faculty for revising the core in the proposed manner." The faculty at Franklin Pierce turned out to be not much different from many others, which, as Sandra Kanter (2000) described, "holds strong beliefs about what students should learn in college, and [whose] discussions about the curriculum inevitably turned into abstract debates about what an educated person should know" (pp. 6–7). John Thelin (2000) writes that some critics of academe "portray curriculum change as a kind of slow, painful death by boredom, a process drawn out over long meetings, finally expiring in the form of tabled motions" (p. 12). These critics were on the mark if we look at the reality at Franklin Pierce. Franklin Pierce College is a progressive four-year residential liberal arts college enrolling about fifteen hundred undergraduates in Rindge, New Hampshire.

NEW DIRECTIONS FOR HIGHER EDUCATION, no. 125, Spring 2004   © Wiley Periodicals, Inc.

In spite of the recommended moratorium, Franklin Pierce pushed ahead with its efforts to reform the curriculum, and indeed a revolution was under way. The inertia was overcome by several critical events. The resignation of one vice president and dean of academic affairs led to the hiring of a new dean, Richard Weeks, who was to provide the necessary leadership to effect real curricular reform. The institution also wanted to distinguish itself from its peer institutions and to begin planning for its own long-term health and growth.

Barriers to Reform

The list of barriers to curricular change included inertia born out of tradition and taking the form of comments along the lines of, "We've been doing it this way for years. What's wrong with that?" or "We've always done it this way, and no one was complaining." A unionized faculty with a strong tradition of autonomy, a penchant for beating the drum of academic freedom, and an inherent distrust of administration engendered a resistance to change imposed from above and made faculty reluctant to move ahead. Fear played a large part in the equation—not just the risks that might be involved regarding turf and the reallocation of resources, but also the risk that comes with having to do something new or different. For an older faculty (the average age in September 1990 was 48.6), who had been at the institution for over a decade (the average term of service at that time was 11.6 years), change meant more work and felt like an indictment of their own abilities in the classroom. They had been working with a distribution system for some thirty years, lecturing in their classes, and no one had said it was "bad." Now they felt they were being called inadequate.

Another significant obstacle had to do with faculty demographics. In 1990, there was a noticeable lack of midrange faculty—those who were not junior and thus had earned some stature on campus but were not senior and prone to be part of the entrenched position. (Faculty who came in at the lowest level of assistant professor typically moved up to full professor at the end of ten years.) Curricular change relies on these midrange faculty to take a leadership position. Their stature keeps them from feeling vulnerable or deciding that the politic thing to do is get along with the "old guard" and thus ensure their tenure, and their newness relative to the old guard makes them more open to change and perhaps less fearful of it.

A lack of institutional self-confidence also created great difficulties too. Franklin Pierce faculty had long heard from students that it was "just Franklin Pierce College" and had bought into this attitude—a sort of, "Well since we're just Franklin Pierce, we couldn't possibly be doing something really great" mentality.

Finances were sure to be a barrier. The new curriculum would require more faculty and faculty development programs to help existing faculty become familiar with active learning pedagogies, writing across the curriculum initiatives, team teaching skills, and how to be interdisciplinary. Whether internally or externally funded, there would be a significant cost to developing, implementing, and sustaining such a program.

The New Curricular Plan

Under the direction of Dean Weeks, a new curricular plan was designed, discussed, and voted on by the faculty in a span of seven months. The original Integrated Core Curriculum consisted of forty-four credit hours. It would be thematic, integrated, sequential, distributed over four years, with component courses required and not elective, and for the most part team-taught and interdisciplinary. The Integrated Core was also designed to feature a collaborative pedagogy, incorporate a community service component, and use portfolio assessment as a means of evaluating both the program and students' personal development.

In early 1991, a core group of interested, committed faculty was appointed by Weeks and the chair of the curriculum committee to the Pierce Plan Committee. This group, which was to lead the process of review and revision of the Pierce Plan prior to its adoption, was heavily weighted toward junior faculty, although it included a few senior faculty members. At its annual spring meeting, the board of trustees approved the new curricular plan, and implementation began immediately. The curriculum transition team (CTT) was appointed and began planning for the implementation of the Pierce Plan. This CTT would "dissolve, when in the judgment of the Dean Weeks, a permanent structure, led by a Pierce Plan Director and including a majority of the component coordinators, can be constituted." The CTT was dissolved in December 1991, and the Core Steering Committee met for the first time on January 15, 1992. During the summer of 1991, the Association of American Colleges and Universities (AAC&U) invited Franklin Pierce College to participate in its Engaging Cultural Legacies program. In addition, two National Endowment for the Humanities grants for faculty development and curriculum design were secured (one grant for the 1991–1992 term and one for the 1993–1994 term), adding cachet and credibility to the new curriculum and allowing for a series of grant-sponsored summer workshops and on-campus visits by various course consultants.

The AAC&U project connected Franklin Pierce with Charlie Reed and North Carolina's Queens College, and the NEH grants allowed us to bring in John Nichols of St. Joseph's College in Indiana to help with course design, development, and implementations. Nichols is a Distinguished Teaching Professor at St. Joseph's and a senior fellow in the Association of American Colleges and Universities Greater Expectations Initiative. Starting in the fall of 1991, pilot sections of the first-year courses were run and assessed, and in the fall of 1992, with much public awareness, a new liberal education core experience began. This curricular reform, called the Pierce

Plan, articulated Franklin Pierce's general education intentions: the Liberal Education Core Requirements

> should foster, to the greatest extent possible, a common liberal education experience for Pierce students. The purpose of this approach is not to promote a common set of conclusions, but to make possible a broad discussion among students and faculty of important issues. The theme of the core program is "The Individual and Community." This theme provides an internal unity to interdisciplinary investigations from many perspectives. . . . All emphasize the acquisition of knowledge and skills that will empower students to attain the Goals of the Franklin Pierce College Experience by the time of graduation. All core courses have significant writing components and opportunities for oral expressions by students. All will endeavor to engage students at their level and bring them to greater academic and intellectual competence.

The Curriculum Ten Years Later: Review and Reform

More than ten years have passed since the Pierce Plan was approved and the pilot sections were run. Two more deans have graced the stage. A provost is now directing the show, and a second core coordinator is in place.

The Individual and Community Integrated Curriculum has all of the components that general education aficionados espouse. It is a common experience required of all students regardless of major and is spread over four years. It constitutes somewhat more than one-third of each student's program for graduation. It has a first-year seminar, for graduation credit, that emphasizes academics, civic engagement, and transition to the institution. This seminar houses the academic advising for first-year students and leverages retention by helping students to make a strong, early connection to a faculty member, a peer group, and the institution. An assessment program for both students and the curriculum itself is in place and has led to curricular innovations. The new curriculum was poised to meet accreditation standards and in fact received high marks from the New England Association of Schools and Colleges in the 1998 visit. There is a senior capstone experience so general education truly encompasses the full scope of the undergraduate experience. The program promotes interdisciplinarity, civic engagement, and active learning. Faculty from a variety of disciplines teach together, design courses together, and learn how to negotiate and cross disciplinary borders. According to student course evaluations, all courses are meeting with the approval of no less than 50 percent of the students enrolled, and most were meeting with a 70 to 80 percent approval rating.

Alongside these positive program outcomes a number of concerns lingered from the program's inception and, in the push for revolution, had remained unresolved. The concerns most often voiced were that the core was too big, too costly to deliver, relied too heavily on adjunct faculty, and did not allow for enough choice; moreover, there was not enough faculty ownership of the core. In April 1999, the vice president and dean of academic affairs, Billy Horton, established the Core Review Committee whose charge was to gather information to assist with a thorough evaluation of the various pieces of the core curriculum—its syllabi, staffing, pedagogy, team teaching, decision making, interdisciplinarity—and an economic analysis of the various methods of delivering the core, including an analysis of the use of part-time and adjunct faculty and disparities in divisional participation in teaching in the core. The committee would act as a recommending body and after a twelve- to eighteen-month review would perhaps propose revisions to the program.

The impetus for this review came from the college's "Northeastern Association of Schools and Colleges (NEASC) Self Study Report" (2000) that made several observations about the performance of the college relative to NEASC Standard 4—Programs and Instruction. (NEASC standards provide guidance for colleges and universities to guide them in the accreditation process.) Among those observations was a concern that Franklin Pierce had not taken enough notice of or done sufficient evaluation to determine the strengths and weaknesses of the integrated curriculum. The self-study also noted concerns that had persisted since the program's beginnings and were contributing to faculty and student frustration with the core. Some of the salient issues were a widespread uncertainty about the purpose and content of the first-year seminar, the inadequacy of resources for faculty development and the hiring of sufficient full-time faculty to staff both the core and the majors, and concerns about the sequencing of courses.

This Core Review Committee began its work in April 1999 and continued through April 2001. An interim report to faculty was presented in August 2000 at the fall faculty workshop. Response from the workshop was reviewed and incorporated into the subsequent work of the committee. A final report was prepared by Horton and presented to the faculty in June 2001. This final report had no specific proposals for revision or change to the Individual and Community Integrated Curriculum.

In August and September 2001, the Core Review Committee reconvened at the request of the newly appointed vice president and provost, Suzanne Buckley. It was time for action. The committee met on August 28 to discuss an action plan and timetable and was asked to decide what Franklin Pierce values and what it can afford for its core and to ensure compliance with NEASC recommendations and requirements. The final goal, according to Buckley in an e-mail to members of the committee on August 21, was to have an "academically excellent, fiscally sound program that complies with NEASC requirements." The recommendations of the August 28 meeting were presented to the college community on September 11, 2001. On-site and on-line forums about the recommendations began on September 21 and concluded on September 26. The Core Review Committee met in early October to review these materials and on October 12, 2001, crafted a final set of recommendations that included the following:

The theme of Individual and Community will remain, be embedded and assessed in courses approved for general education. The total number of program credits will be 38.

1. Senior Liberal Arts course is to be eliminated
2. Portfolio Assessment Seminar is to be eliminated.

Portfolio Assessment exercises and Capstone reflection will be embedded in redesigned, existing upper level courses.

3. The Social Science Division will create a new course based on a combination of the existing two Science of Society courses or continue to offer both courses. Students will select one Social Science course for a total of three credits.
4. The Business Division will create and offer one course. The course will include social science methodology and subject matter, for instance, inclusion of macro economic issues.
5. Three versions of IC101 will remain.
6. College Writing I and II will remain.
7. Natural Science will be maintained at eight credit hours.
8. Foundations of Math will remain for three credits.
9. The Arts will be maintained at three credit hours. Experiencing the Arts will be replaced with a menu of three courses. This menu could include Experiencing the Arts.
10. Humanities will be increased from six credit hours to nine with a menu of six courses. This menu could include American Experience, Twentieth Century, Ancient and Medieval Worlds, Reason and Romanticism, and Philosophy and Religion classes.

This set of recommendations was presented simultaneously to the Core Steering Committee and the Curriculum Committee. The Core Steering Committee was unable to come to any consensus with respect to the recommendations and settled for a series of individual comments on various portions of the recommendations. The Curriculum Committee agreed to the revisions proposed by the Core Review Committee and the provost made the formal announcement of the changes on December 12, 2001.

A Core Implementation Committee was appointed and began the work with a re-visioning of the existing Fifteen Goals of the Student Experience. These goals were distilled and compressed into three overarching "Goals of the Student Experience," given the acronym "TeaCH," which represents:

1. Tolerance and Community: Be able to articulate their own attitudes and values and recognize the persistent tensions between self and community; demonstrate understanding and respect for views and cultures differing from their own by working collaboratively and participating in community affairs.

2. Content Literacy and Integration with Critical Analysis: Be effective writers and speakers, combine a mastery of pertinent mathematics with knowledge of the methods and aims of modern science, and be adept at using modern information resources. Students should have a substantive understanding of the way artistic expression, historical, natural and cultural contexts in a global setting shape and enrich our communities and our individual lives. Students should become active participants and leaders in their communities, with a developed sense of ethics that encourages civility, tolerance for differences, and a commitment to a life of collaborative work and learning.

3. Holistic Preparation for Leadership and Lifelong Learning: Be able to seek and apply knowledge in a holistic manner for the rest of their lives and to serve as responsible citizens and leaders in local, regional and global communities.

Following months of discussion, commentary, and reworking not only by the Core Implementation Committee but also the teaching faculty, faculty voted on February 12, 2003, to replace the existing fifteen goals with these three goals. These TeaCH goals would apply to the entire Franklin Pierce College experience and would not refer just to the goals of the Individual and Community Integrated Curriculum. They would be institutional goals—goals of both the core and the majors. In response to these goals, each of the Individual and Community Integrated Curriculum components revamped its component goals to reflect and amplify these TeaCH goals.

All this has been accomplished as a prelude to more comprehensive, effective institutional review and assessment. The other details of implementation—new administrative structures, new course development, on-line assessment, and portfolios—are in process with the hope of piloting new courses in the 2003–2004 term to better align with the revised goals and help create a more meaningful experience for students. Two courses will be phased out with certain components of the courses adopted in existing courses. In addition, new senior capstones in the majors will be revised to better integrate the majors and the Individual and Community Curriculum. There is much work to be done, and undoubtedly additional negotiation and conversations will occur.

Conclusion

In the light of the more than ten years of curricular reform at Franklin Pierce, we have seen revolution followed by evolution; a large-scale overhaul of a long-existing distribution program occurred and in the years that followed, small-scale tweaking of the new Individual and Community Integrated Curriculum became the norm. When the curriculum was assessed in a holistic way nearly ten years later, the resulting curricular reforms were relatively modest. Recommendations for more sweeping changes (among them, reducing the humanities requirement to six credits or the natural science requirement to year credits, dropping the Individual and Community theme, or jettisoning the first-year seminar) were not supported by the faculty and in fact proved to be rather contentious. The Core Review Committee, and the faculty as well, settled for small, politically less painful recommendations.

Although it is not yet clear what is to come and whether the newest iteration of the Individual and Community Integrated Curriculum will be successful, I must admit that in my role as core coordinator, I am plagued by mixed feelings. I am saddened by the proposed elimination of the sophomore and senior general education-specific courses (portfolio assessment and senior liberal arts seminar), and I am concerned about whether a new administrative structure that houses the Individual and Community Integrated Curriculum courses in the academic divisions will promote ownership as is intended. I worry about how coherence will be maintained, what sort of sequencing options might develop, and that the writing across the curriculum efforts will be for naught. I worry about maintaining a distinctive, credible program. I could spend a great deal of time or energy dwelling on these worries, but I have chosen not to do so and instead take solace in the fact that all curricular reform is ongoing and that nothing about our curriculum must be etched in stone unless we as a faculty choose to do so. On September 29, 1993, Ernest Boyer, who at that time was the president of the Carnegie Foundation for the Advancement of Teaching, spoke to the faculty, staff, and students of Franklin Pierce College on the issue of "Individualism and the Community." In his address, he remarked on our new curricular program:

> What you have created here, it seems to me, is an essential conversation. . . . There is no single way by which integration must occur. There are literally dozens of models that can stir vital inquiry within the academy. . . . While there is no single way for colleges to resolve the general education question, what I fear most is that we might stop debating it. Because in the end the greatest value of debating general education is not in the certainty of the outcome, but in the quality of the discourse. . . . I hope you continue the debate understanding that the virtue is in the continued search for larger meanings.

Curricular reform is never easy, and in my experience there is no one-size-fits-all model to pass along. Moreover, truly exceptional programs are not static but able to change over time just as an institution changes. I want to underscore the necessity and benefit of the process itself, the inclusion of all constituencies on campus, the need for good civil communication, and a willingness to work collaboratively. Curricular reform is difficult. It is frustrating, and much of the time it is agonizingly slow and incremental. You may periodically think you truly dislike some of your colleagues. Maybe you do. You will question your sanity, and perhaps with good reason. In the end, you will not be able to satisfy everyone, but you will be able to craft a program that maintains your institution's mission and professes your institution's values—if you can articulate that mission and those values. As you emerge from the process, you will anticipate and appreciate the evolving nature of general education. And maybe another revolution will not be necessary.

References

Franklin Pierce College. "NEASC Self Study Report." Unpublished study, 2000.

Kanter, S. "Reflections on Reform." *Peer Review,* Summer 2000, pp. 4–8.

Thelin, J. "A Legacy of Lethargy?" *Peer Review,* Summer 2000, pp. 9–14.

SARAH T. DANGELANTONIO is a professor of English and the coordinator of Individual and Integrated Curriculum and Writing Programs at Franklin Pierce College.

3

How do evolving academic priorities influence the review and reform of a pioneering general education program?

The Reforms in General Education at American University

Haig Mardirosian

If general education programs purport to embrace a universe of knowledge, at least a universe as defined by a particular institution, then in practical terms, they must also reflect widespread sanction, sustenance, and supervision within the institution. In practice, such programs are interdisciplinary and inhabit interjurisdictional surroundings. In order to review or alter such programs, the academic community must look past traditional boundaries and old antagonisms to the contemporary realities that shape an institution's academic affairs.

Origins of American University's General Education Program

American University in Washington, D.C., is a private, comprehensive, selective, Carnegie Doctoral Extensive institution. Many of its students come from all fifty of the United States, and more than 15 percent call some 150 other nations home. Most are drawn to Washington, D.C., for the obvious benefits of place, the plentiful possibility of public sector studies and connections, and internships and other experience-based programming considered both essential and excellent. American University students generally sit to the left of center in their political views and are likely to volunteer for community service, the Peace Corps, or Habitat for Humanity. They rally to opportunities for service and real-world experience at high levels of government, politics, and the media. Furthermore, they count on the immediate and palpable linkage of such experience to their classroom and campus life.

NEW DIRECTIONS FOR HIGHER EDUCATION, no. 125, Spring 2004 © Wiley Periodicals, Inc.

Six schools and colleges comprise the university: the College of Arts and Sciences, the Kogod School of Business, the School of Communication, the School of International Service, the School of Public Affairs, and the Washington College of Law. All except the law school offer undergraduate instruction.

American University was an early adopter of what most would consider the classic archetype of general education: value-, goal-, and objective-oriented courses arranged into five broad curricular areas representing the universe of human knowledge. These areas are coherently tied into sequential clusters, and proceed from broad foundational experience to more specific inquiry. For all the deliberate structural detail, the framers of the American University program nonetheless sought to safeguard choice and flexibility for the university's five thousand or so undergraduates. From its launch in 1989, the program has proved both intellectually and structurally durable, even against a scenario of considerable institutional change and growth.

Rarely do widespread curricular reforms grow out of thin air. At American University, administrators equated reforming general education with enhancing the quality of undergraduate learning. Faculty designed the program in the mid- and late 1980s under the direction of the dean of academic development and founding general education director, Ann R. Ferren. Ferren drew together divergent university constituencies and interests by mooring the task at hand to the university senate and its committees charged with academic oversight. The senate, in turn, established the General Education Committee specifically composed of senior (and therefore presumably steadfast and wise) faculty members. The mandate put before the community rang simple: improve the academic rigor and coherency of undergraduate education at American University. The response engaged the entire community in serious discussion, debate, and unprecedented levels of faculty development, faculty service, and curricular advancement. In two and a half years, from early 1987 to fall 1989, 150 courses, nearly 80 percent of them entirely new or substantially revised existing ones, found their way through an all-embracing approval process, were banded into more than forty cohesive clusters, and appeared in the catalogue.

Curricular Areas

Although scholars can organize the whole of human knowledge in myriad ways, American University's general education schema divided learning into five expansive segments and fitted courses from across the colleges and schools into the appropriate areas:

Area 1, The Creative Arts: Art; computer science and information systems; philosophy; literature; performing arts

Area 2, Traditions That Shaped the Western World: Art; history; Jewish studies; language and foreign studies; physics; philosophy; literature; American studies; justice, law, and society; anthropology; communications; psychology; sociology; government

Area 3, The International and Intercultural Experience: Anthropology; language and foreign studies; philosophy; international studies; sociology; economics; literature; history; government; communications; international business

Area 4, Social Institutions and Behaviors: Anthropology; American studies; history; sociology; women's and gender studies; economics; finance; government; communications; philosophy; psychology; education; health and fitness; justice, law, and society

Area 5, The Natural Sciences: Biology; anthropology; chemistry; health and fitness; psychology; physics

Early in the formative process, the university committed itself to front-line teaching and resources sufficient to its general education teaching mission. "Front-line" teaching denoted full-time professorial course staffing. With 545 full-time teaching faculty members attached to the six colleges and schools, the overall campus teaching ethos warranted some consideration. Professors who pictured their role, expertise, purpose, and passion as aimed at graduate training or upper-level undergraduate lecturing faced the not insignificant question of how to educate predominantly first- and second-year students successfully without resorting to formulaic solutions.

Large, impersonal lectures, except in specific and deliberate circumstances, could not suffice as the "one-size-fits-all" key to general education. Neither could "introduction to the discipline" courses if they skirted unalloyed the program's values, goals, and learning objectives. Those central goals and objectives, either program-wide or attached to specific curricular areas, saw to it that no viewpoint could lay claim to the whole answer or that no course or discipline was a territory sufficient unto itself without need of stretching past its own limits. What were these objectives?

Institutional Values, Goals, and Learning Objectives

With consultation from the whole faculty, the General Education Committee articulated six major objectives that would not only touch but also consciously influence courses in the program:

- Writing experience to enhance basic communication skills
- A critical thinking component to enhance the ability to make and analyze judgments based on reasoning and evidence
- Recognition of the ethical issues pertinent to the field or discipline
- Development of quantitative and computing skills

- Development of intuitive, creative, and aesthetic faculties and the ability to connect these with reasoning skills
- Attention to a variety of perspectives, including those perspectives that emerge from new scholarship on gender, race, and class as well as from non-Western cultural traditions

   Faculty members from each of the five curricular areas also collaborated in enunciating area-specific goals. These specialized objectives covered the essentials of inquiry into the area's disciplines. Taken together, the program-wide and area objectives certified that American University's model of general education would be distinctive, that it would convey the mind and character of the university, that it would bring students to a fuller grasp of a complex, fast, and shrinking world, and that pedagogy and classroom environment would, of necessity, change. Faculty could choose to stay put with erstwhile exemplars of teaching, of undivided dedication to major and graduate education, of hide-bound disciplinary limits, or they could purposefully reevaluate teaching mission and style.

Curricular Reform: Impact and Lingering Questions

Large-scale curricular modernizations often bring serendipitous and unpremeditated benefits. For all the off-putting sniping, squabbling, posturing, and sophistry, curricular debates almost always advance institutional goals and help focus emerging mission and common purpose. American University had to mull over the effect of a thirty-credit-hour general education load on its majoring programs and on students increasingly enamored with double majors, major-minor combinations, internships, and opportunities to study abroad. (An additional nine credit hours of university-wide requirements, two semesters of college writing and one semester of finite mathematics (or above), puts the sum of undergraduate requirements at thirty-nine hours before counting a major or minor, although six credits of general education may count toward a specific major.) In founding the program, the university had to allow for stringent professional accreditation standards in individual professional disciplines (like business). It had to overcome student perceptions that general education amounted to a rigid knot of regulations meant to throttle choice, creativity, credit for prior experience, or interest. It had to demonstrate that general education contributed significantly toward possibilities for a career or job. It had to reenergize senior faculty, co-opt their leadership and wisdom, and recruit new faculty capable of the masterful teaching and intellectual scope vital to invigorating the general education classroom. It had to match its intellectual commitment to general education with concomitant resource allocation policies and practices in times of both relative scarcity and plenty.

These figured to be crucial issues in the fall of 1989 as students first entered American University's general education classrooms. How did American University fare in the decade following, and how did the program develop and experience further reformation?

Program Assessment as Prelude to Review and Reform

Projects like general education are magnets for continuous appraisal. General education directors and boards thrive on gathering and interpreting data, in part because such knowledge arms them for dealing with deans and department chairs, governing bodies, and administration, but also because the underlying conventions of general education demand it. The assertion that attention to students' writing skills should take prominence in a general education course, for instance, necessitates validation down the road. General education programs must assess themselves and must do so continually.

From the outset, American University's General Education Program left the door open to curricular revision. Variables like staffing, shifts in departmental emphasis and expertise, curriculum innovation, and prospects of refining and improving general education stipulated some degree of course changes and reclustering. Many faculty members, however, distrusted the established process, calling it cumbersome and bureaucratic. Because of the 150-course ceiling mandated by the university senate, no proposals, no matter how innovative or worthwhile, could be accepted into the program unless others were retired. It is no wonder that general education directors sneaked out on curricular search-and-destroy missions in hopes of finding chronically underenrolled or poorly evaluated courses in their crosshairs.

As for new courses, faculty innovators steered their proposals through a two-year, five-tiered curriculum approval process with layer upon layer of consultation, feedback, and approval. Teaching unit heads and faculty councils, college deans and their educational policy committees, the general education director and committee, the university senate and its Undergraduate Studies Committee, and finally the provost each played a role in the approval procedure. Some faculty responded with subtle and clever subterfuge. Courses sometimes may have drifted in focus because of faculty staffing or shifts of interest, but also because some instructors chose to skirt the administrative barriers to change. A course entitled "Japan and the US," for example, became in practice "Japan, China, and the US," a change eventually discovered in routine syllabus review and sanctioned by appropriate committee action.

Furthermore, deans, chairs, and faculty members grew aware that general education enrollments influenced resource allocation significantly (indeed, many a small, archetypal college major had been rescued, if not completely reinvigorated, through its firm and extensive commitment to

general education teaching). Whereas departments once argued against
increasing their effort, the academic culture had begun to change. It was
clearly in the interest of academic units to preserve and cultivate their general education offerings. Offering more course sections or more seats in an
existing section, actions requiring general education office approval, meant
the likelihood of attracting a greater share of student registrations and gain-
ing a competitive advantage against other units. Still, despite the incentives
for change, both as arguable intellectual necessity and temporal reward, the
administrative barriers to change proved formidable enough to prevent
the program from major renewal. In ten years, only sixteen new courses had
been introduced to the program, a hair over 10 percent.

Overall, students embraced the purposes of the program and, in particular, applauded the outstanding teaching in it, but they voiced increasing frustration with what they saw as restrictive and arbitrary course
clustering. A few students argued that courses were not suitably rigorous;
more asserted that courses were *too* rigorous. The university's exit survey
of students rated the program somewhere near the seventieth percentile.
The glass was certainly more than half full, but even a third of respondents
claiming less satisfaction with general education than with majors or minors
intimated a need for action.

Faculty agreed that some course choices and pairings reflected the arbitrary patterns of political dealing more than unsullied scholarly uprightness.
Faculty also supported goals and outcomes with virtually no complaint
(after all, they had been instrumental in authoring these), but a small number of teachers seemingly ignored these in their classes. Even that phenomenon carried a message. The objective of requiring students to write had
been attached to foundation courses, which are typically more heavily
enrolled than second-level courses. Faculty ignoring the mandates on writing work therefore validated complaints that work load was disproportion-
ately heavy in general education foundation courses. Foundation course
enrollments have typically been forty students as compared to second-level
average enrollments of thirty-two.

Faculty Development and Resources

To help faculty meet the demands of teaching general education courses
well, the general education program proposed and found funds for a
General Education Faculty Assistance Program (GEFAP), which enabled
faculty to request small cash grants to pay hourly wages to undergraduate
and graduate teaching assistants of their own choosing. The point was simple: innovative teaching, especially in heavily enrolled classes, often requires
inventive techniques such as tutorials, discussions, simulations, and a broad
array of distance learning and allied technologies. Developing such innovation stipulates time and support. Furthermore, many pioneering learning
techniques are best dispensed from nontraditional and nonauthoritarian

sources. Student-to-student learning would best suit many of these new pedagogical purposes. Some teaching units, especially larger ones, already had graduate teaching fellows deployed in support of general education, but others did not. GEFAP would make available even-handed access to teaching help.

Given the budget and cost of student part-time wages, from twenty-seven to forty assistants have been funded for up to sixty hours of work per semester, a number representing between 10 and 13 percent of all course sections. In seven years of providing GEFAP assistants to faculty teaching general education courses, the number of applications has increased with regularity. The magnitude of that increase has reflected overall trends in undergraduate enrollment. Thus, faculty members have come to regard GEFAP as a beneficial tool in personalizing uncongenial large classes while student evaluations of teaching have consistently disclosed higher levels of satisfaction with courses staffed by GEFAP assistants.

GEFAP guidelines do not sanction busywork, errand running, or grading of undergraduates by undergraduates. However, nongraded peer evaluation is both appropriate and encouraged. Commentary on writing drafts, for instance, constitutes appraisal and contributes significantly to the improved quality of student writing in general, but it does not directly entail the origination of a grade.

Just as students must evaluate faculty teaching in each course, they must also evaluate GEFAP assistants. These assessments tender a valuable glimpse into classroom activities. They also detect problems or misunderstandings in the use of GEFAP time. GEFAP evaluations and anecdotal feedback have furthermore certified that the best GEFAP assistants are students who have previously taken the course, not so much because they know the course material or even the style and demands of the instructor, but because they have insights into process and mode of inquiry typical of the discipline. Remarkably, GEFAP assistants often come from majors outside the field in which they serve, a reality strengthening the interdisciplinary filaments of general education. Students accept the credibility, for instance, of a nonscience major serving as a laboratory assistant or a nonmusician coaching them on hearing patterns in a Bach fugue. The temptation to shunt aside offers of help predicated on the suspicion that "you understand it because you have prior talent or experience" vanishes.

Yet another faculty development innovation has bettered the quality of general education teaching at American University. In response to a call from its strategic plan, the university established the Center for Teaching Excellence (CTE). The center amassed a range of established faculty development agendas and, together with the university's academic computing enterprise (branded "e-Academics"), adjoined learning and teaching technology to its activities. While the mission of the center never specified particular programs or levels of instruction, faculty members teaching general education courses were obvious clients. By academic year 2001–2002, the center together with e-Academics had arranged for every American University course to be automatically authorized for use of on-line teaching technology. (While any number of courses may choose to employ e-mail, listservs, or class Web pages, the teaching technology of choice at American University has been Blackboard. Courses were set up in "passive mode," meaning that nothing would appear in course listings on-line at American University sites or the Blackboard site until individual faculty chose to activate the account.) By fall 2001, the CTE reckoned that more than 25 percent of all courses were actively using on-line distance-learning techniques routinely, that countless more relied on e-mail as a primary means of communication between instructors and students, and that a significant number of these sections were indeed general education courses. Of general education course sections in fall 2001, forty-seven, or 26 percent, were active Blackboard users.

A Reassessment from the Ground Up

A decade in the life of any academic program can amount to an eternity. Owing to institutional and market shifts and reallocation, student demographics, expectations of accrediting bodies, and the prevalent motivation of the academic community to embrace advancement, any program can safely presuppose periodic study and possible reform sooner rather than later. At American University, the call for further examination of the general education program came at the ten-year mark in academic year 1999–2000. It was an opportune moment coinciding with other institutional planning milestones: the final two years of strategic plan implementation, the presidential conversations with the university community regarding the institution's future, and an upcoming accreditation by the Middle States Association of Colleges and Schools for which evidence of institutional assessment work was crucial.

The provost, Cornelius M. Kerwin, in consultation with university senate leaders, entrusted the general education review to a committee drawn equally from the General Education Committee and from faculty and staff representing constituencies with a stake in general education. These included students and faculty from each of the undergraduate schools and colleges, as well as the Student Confederation, registrar, dean of students, International Student Services, Enrollment Services, Office of Institutional Research, the University Library, and the general education program itself. During 2000–2001, the committee amassed data including surveys of student and alumni attitudes about the general education program (a questionnaire prepared and administered by the General Education Office went to current students in second-level general education courses, graduating seniors, and alumni from the class of 1995, one of the earliest classes to have graduated after the implementation of the current curriculum in

1989–1990), results of student and faculty focus groups, transcripts of student and faculty town meetings, reports of faculty and administrative attitudes from individual schools and colleges, and a wealth of existing and updated institutional data concerning curriculum, enrollment patterns, and course staffing.

General education programs may stand or fall on their perceived meaning and coherence. Recognizing this, the review committee put special emphasis on the particular relationship of intellectual and structural matters. The critics of the program complained about the lack of consistency between courses. They alleged that political covenants among units resulted in the curricular decisions that were the basis of the program. They pointed out that not all sections of a given general education course necessarily met program objectives and standards uniformly.

However, the review committee concluded that few, if any, of these criticisms justified hefty program redesign. A general education comprising five curricular areas, each offering foundational and second-level courses, connected across disciplinary and college boundaries, and united around intellectual themes, institutional values, and learning objectives, remained sound and current. But the review team also concluded that several questions demanded attention:

• Foundation and second-level course linkages needed new justification and renewal. Course drift, staffing changes, and curricular innovation since the inception of the program corroborated critics' protests about the validity of linkages. Nothing suggested, however, that the problem was political, only a matter of curricular evolution.

• Program values, goals, and learning objectives still reflected the characteristics of modern society and the world, but they needed updating in order to conform to the university's priorities and planning and to refine their focus. Strategic planning and institutional mission had come to recognize globalism and information literacy as new institutional emphases. How would these be reflected in the general education objectives?

• Courses had to be reexamined. Were they communicating the essential disciplinary content and mode of thought? Did they link validly within the cluster? Had they grown old? Were they rigorous? Was pedagogy up to date? Did they meet program objectives and goals?

• General education staffing and resources needed to service current enrollment patterns. In particular, attention needed to be given to some units where courses were chronically taught by adjunct faculty. (The university had depicted its commitment of excellent teaching in general education in the regulation that no more than 30 percent of general education courses overall, and in each college, school, or department, could be taught by other than full-time faculty.)

• Faculty and student enthusiasm about general education needed to be reinvigorated.

The General Education Review Committee made several dozen recommendations clustered around these themes to the provost and the university senate for approval and implementation.

Given the fast-paced change of institutional priorities and planning and the sometimes serendipitous vagaries of organizational behavior, parts of the implementation began to take on their own life. For instance, the committee tagged the seemingly innocuous and arguably good notion of reestablishing a university-wide advising council—a group bringing together the university's professional advising community with others having a stake in advising—as a necessary but second-priority task. However, the university president, concluding his "Campus Conversations" planning process, called for a renovation of academic advising (as one of fifteen organizational and academic improvements). This encouraged immediate action on advising reform, pushing beyond the specific scope general education reform. Likewise, a learning resources project team, envisioned in the general education review as a means of delivering improved academic support to the program, became part of grander institutional priorities. In this way, different initiatives across the university conspired to mold and modify those undertaken under the banner of general education reform.

Reviewing Courses and Creating New Clusters

The course appraisal mandated by the review committee proceeded as the university senate began its debate over other aspects of the overall program design. Thus, the basis for course realignment, new or redesigned clusters, and even the association of a course with the program in the first place, would be in hand at the same time that other innovations would be implemented. Course reviews consumed time. Each faculty member teaching general education courses was asked to contribute to the self-study, an assessment guided by a template of questions about the course, its association with other courses in the cluster, its approbation of technology and other pedagogical enhancements, and its concinnity with program values, goals, and learning objectives, both existing and proposed. The results of that assessment not only yielded a rich profile of general education teaching practices and pedagogies, a database already stout with information gleaned from course syllabi, but also was the primary apparatus by which the General Education Committee could make decisions about new course clustering.

The review committee had specifically suggested that the present "tight" course clusters be replaced by new "loose" clusters. That is, previously a student enrolling in any one of seven to ten foundation courses in a curricular area would be obliged to select subsequently from six or seven corresponding second-level courses of the area. Under the revised provisions, a student could take one of several foundations, any of which would lead to as many as a dozen second-level courses. Such clustering would give students lateral advantage in choosing foundation courses. The hope was that students could find the foundations courses appealing destinations themselves rather than prerequisites to hoped-for second-level courses. In order to reckon such new alignments, the General Education Committee clearly drew on the facts disclosed in the course review.

The Future: General Education and the University College

The latest iteration of academic planning has spawned a vision of a new pan-undergraduate foundation defined as the "university college." The college is intended to further impress the institution's core values on students during their first two years of study. Although thought about a university college remains nascent, some outcomes are predictable. General education will likely have a central place in such an all-embracing undergraduate enterprise. Under the most recent reforms, general education's value and objective-based curricular methods have grown to affect the whole of the undergraduate core. A university college at some level would reinforce the strengths of the reforms already in place, and it would make general education's intrinsic indisciplinarity even more integral to students' overall experience.

Academic and student life planners alike look to experiential learning and common student experience as key elements of a vibrant undergraduate program. As these emerging rudiments chew up more and more turf that had belonged strictly to the habitual academic empire, so learning activities have invaded the province of student life, once the realm of counselors, housing officials, Greek advisers, and chaplains. Overreaching the boundaries of learning denotes far more than purging the ramparts between academic units and faculty eager to do interdisciplinary work.

General education programs like that of American University devised the notion of learning and teaching unbridled by the tether of any single academic unit, another way of saying that all are engaged and thus all claim some ownership. The next phase of evolution as avowed in such innovations as university colleges, enhanced experiential learning opportunities, common experience courses, college life seminars, and residential life and learning programming guarantees that the faith and aspirations of the general education model will penetrate learning even further.

Though still a work in progress, American University's reformation and review of its model of general education has taken a step toward a broader, cohesive, and universal plan for all its undergraduate students. The American University program insinuates that general education in the twenty-first century might well be termed comprehensive education.

HAIG MARDIROSIAN is associate dean of academic affairs, director of the general education program, and professor of music at American University in Washington, D.C.

4

*Few are challenged to create a general education
curriculum for a new college, applying best practices
while achieving articulation and accreditation of the
program.*

Cascadia Community College: Finding the "Cascadia Way"

Victoria Muñoz Richart

Not often is there a chance to build a general education curriculum from
scratch. That is exactly what we did at Cascadia Community College in
Bothell, thirteen miles north of Seattle, Washington. It was an opportunity to incorporate the best that research on students, curriculum design,
and teaching and learning could offer. Yet we needed to develop a general
education program—indeed an entire community college curriculum—
within the context of some very conventional forces. This chapter
describes how the general education program at Cascadia came about and
what we learned along the way.

The Beginning

In early 1990, a Washington State master plan study revealed that the greatest projected number of underserved students was on the northeast shores
of Lake Washington, thirteen miles from Seattle. In that same year, the
University of Washington (UW) opened a branch campus in temporary
quarters in Bothell. This was one of five public university branch campuses
established by the legislature that year to provide time- and place-bound
students with upper-division undergraduate studies.

In 1994, the state legislature created Cascadia Community College,
recognizing the growing need for a comprehensive community college in
the region. Cascadia and the University of Washington, Bothell, also were
to share the same campus location and, to the extent possible, were to share
services. The governor appointed a five-member board of trustees for the
community college.

NEW DIRECTIONS FOR HIGHER EDUCATION, no. 125, Spring 2004 © Wiley Periodicals, Inc.

The enabling legislation provided funding only for planning the college. During this time, the college consisted of the interim president, one assistant, and one architect. Working with the board, they established the college's mission, policies on institutional governance and a facilities master plan, and negotiated arrangements with nearby Shoreline Community College to serve as Cascadia's initial fiscal agent and parent institution. The Cascadia board and the planning staff reviewed best educational practices and commissioned the design of the new college's facilities, site location, and colocation development with its UW partner.

The Mission

Cascadia's mission that emerged from this period of planning was an ambitious, exciting, and challenging one: "Cascadia Community College will be an exemplar of the 21st century community college, a learner centered, comprehensive, culturally rich, and technologically advanced learning and teaching institution, which emphasizes student achievement and educational excellence, seamlessly linked with the community area enterprise, and other educational institutions." This mission guided the creation of all college operations and each course of study. But before we could have programs, we needed facilities, interinstitutional arrangements for the acceptance of students who wished to transfer and continue their education at a baccalaureate-granting institution, and initial accreditation for programs.

In 1998, construction began for the new campus colocated with the UW Bothell, and following a national search, the first permanent president was selected. This was an incredibly busy time at the college as key personnel were hired, buildings arose, the curriculum was designed, and first linkages with the various communities of the district were established. By the fall of 1999, Cascadia was offering continuing education classes, and a year later, Cascadia opened its new doors to credit and noncredit students, offering a full range of career and academic transfer in its new facility. From three employees in 1998, the college has grown to over 275 employees, and has exceeded all enrollment projections, serving over twenty-five hundred students in 2002. It is within that context of beginning, planning, and growth that the general education curriculum came into being. Meeting statewide guidelines governing the recognition, acceptance, and transfer of general education course work was a necessary, albeit conventional, factor in creating this new curriculum.

Academic Statewide Guidelines and Policies

Cascadia's general education program needed not only to meet the standards for regional accreditation but also to comply with state policy regarding transfer of credits. The Higher Education Coordinating Board oversees all of higher education in the state of Washington and provides planning, coordination, monitoring, and policy analysis. Germane to this discussion is the Policy on Inter-College Transfer and Articulation, which governs the transfer of students and the credits they have earned between the public institutions of higher education in the state. For their part, the colleges and universities of Washington have long recognized the importance of easing the transfer of students from one institution to another. Working both directly, college-to-college, and through voluntary associations, such as the Inter-College Relations Commission, they founded mutually acceptable guidelines and procedures for student transfer. Private (independent) institutions work in similar bilateral ways to facilitate transfer of community college students to their institutions.

Also governing general education in the state is the direct transfer agreement (DTA) developed by the Inter-College Relations Commission to facilitate the transfer of students attaining the associate degree or equivalents. These guidelines specify a distributional system of general education course work that sets parameters for the development of general education programs such that we were to design at Cascadia. The DTA associate degree contains ninety quarter-hours of lower-division credit, sixty of them in general education courses. The DTA plan for general education is further subdivided into basic requirements and distribution requirements as follows:

Basic requirements, which include communication skills (ten credits), quantitative and symbolic reasoning skills (five credits), and intermediate algebra proficiency
Distribution requirements: humanities (fifteen to twenty credits), social sciences (fifteen to twenty credits), natural sciences (fifteen to twenty credits), and electives

Student using the DTA associate degree to meet general education requirements need to earn at least a cumulative grade point average of 2.00. Remedial courses (those numbered below 100) are not included in the DTA associate degree.

Cascadia's new curriculum needed to meet the basic general education guidelines and policies of the state. It also needed to fulfill the standards for general education, transfer of credits, and assessment of program set by the Northwest Association of Schools, Colleges and Universities. The challenge was to be innovative and to create the best learning environment for student learning and success within those parameters.

Deriving the Design Principles

While existing colleges and universities often can draw on years of experience and volumes of institutional research on their students and their programs, Cascadia was a new institution. It was also not bound by politics and loyalties of existing programs, policies, and practices. As a learning organization, grounding practice in the good research and the knowledge of what works in college made good sense (Richart, 1998). Thus, we turned to pertinent literature on teaching and learning, on students in college, and on curricular design and effectiveness for guidance in crafting the new curriculum.

Early in 1999, we established the Curriculum and Learning Design Team (CLDT), comprising four newly hired faculty members, and charged it with the development of the general education curriculum. The resulting "Steps to Student Success," Cascadia "Learning Model," and "Student Learning Outcomes" are graphically described on the college's Web site (www.cascadia.ctc.edu). The team was assisted by the president of the college and the college academic administrators, as well as by Ruth Stiehl of the University of Oregon, who served as consultant. Stiehl is coauthor (with Les Lewchuk) of *The Outcomes Primer: Reconstructing the College Curriculum* (2000), and her work gave great guidance to the project, particularly in focusing the new curriculum on outcomes and competencies rather than credits and seat time as indicators of student success.

Underprepared Students. CLDT and the administrative team began by considering students not fully prepared to undertake collegiate-level work. Some students do not receive sufficient preparation in secondary schools to succeed in collegiate studies. Others have been away from education for several years, and as working adults find that knowledge and skills have changed dramatically. Many are first-generation students coming from homes where neither parents, nor brothers and sisters, nor peers have been to college and therefore cannot provide guidance in navigating successfully to complete personal, career, or academic goals.

As a new community college, Cascadia needed to determine how it would address curricular offerings for underprepared students. It found abundant evidence at all educational levels (K–16) that underprepared and minority students continue to face enormous barriers, often being relegated to unchallenging and irrelevant remedial courses. Conventional approaches to remediation often increase the time and expense needed for students to complete their studies and often marginalize them in the process (Dilworth and Robinson, 1995). Cascadia needed to create culturally responsive courses using pedagogy appropriate for the underprepared, enhancing their learning experience, and providing them with a breadth of understanding that was appropriately enabling.

From the research, the CLDT and the administrative team learned of important characteristics that programs successful in targeting at-risk students held in common. Racial, ethnic, linguistic, and other differences were seen as assets on which courses were built rather than employing a conventional deficit model that began with real or imagined weaknesses of students, society, or the community (Dilworth and Robinson, 1995).

We believed that socially conscious curricular restructuring would increase equity and access for students. Uri Treisman at the University of

California, Berkeley, has found that project-based collaborative learning is a powerful means of engaging students who have not performed well in traditional instructional settings. "Disadvantaged" students at Berkeley often failed basic science and math courses. Treisman placed these students in workshop settings, challenged them with problems more complex than those found in standard courses, fostered study groups, urged them to set high expectations, and helped them see that they could achieve success and learn "the unspoken wisdom of excellence." The students in his program produced levels of achievement rivaling those of traditional students in the university (Garland and Treisman, 1993; Treisman, 1994). Drawing on research and good practices, Cascadia's precollegiate curriculum was designed to promote inclusion and access. Precollegiate and general education needed to be closely articulated in the most positive, reaffirming, and engaging manner.

What to Learn. A key question in the fashioning of general education is, "What should all students learn and know?" In a community college, general education programs need to serve both those transferring to four-year undergraduate programs and those in technical, professional, and career programs. To approach this question, the CLDT and the administrative team reviewed literature on how students regard their own learning and what the social expectations would be for which they should be prepared. The research indicated that information age workers would need to spend at least 20 percent of their day engaged in learning, so students should become extremely facile in their learning mechanisms to remain competitive in the global market. Students' knowledge, skills, and abilities should prepare them for their next career and enable them to move between careers and be proficient in civic and personal matters as well. General education needed to be cast broadly in defining what to learn. Also, Cascadia would need to focus on customer satisfaction as a hallmark of an effective program, as would the students on entering the workforce. For them to persist, succeed, and attain their goals and for employers to seek them out and offer them career opportunities, Cascadia's programs needed to be engaging and relevant (Case, 1995; Freiberg and Freiberg, 1996; Hammer and Champy, 1993; McIntyre, 1996; Rifkin, 1995; Rowley, Lujan, and Dolence, 1997; Simsek and Louis, 1994; Weisbord, 1992; Zemsky, 1994).

Nationally, changes in the organization of work have been increasing the demand for workers with higher levels of skill development. This has been true for both technical and nontechnical skills and for all types of workers. The 1991 report by the U.S. Department of Labor, Secretary's Commission on Achieving Necessary Skills (SCANS) concluded that "good jobs will increasingly depend on people who can put knowledge to work" (U.S. Department of Labor, 1991). This included proficiencies in basic skills (reading, writing, computation, listening, speaking), along with the ability to think creatively, collaborate, and adapt readily to changes in their work, including technological changes; such skills are crucial in a global economy

(U.S. Department of Labor, 1991). The CLDT used the SCANS report as a touchstone for defining general education goals, identifying and integrating key competencies into the curriculum, and selecting instructional strategies intended to strengthen the skills of adults in daily life and the workplace. We concluded that the ability to communicate, especially with people from other cultures, was crucial for all students. The global worker's preparation requires a curriculum that promotes understanding of cultural, social, and political differences and enhances common values and shared insights. This training necessarily includes the development of interpersonal skills that will enhance the worker's ability to participate, form, and lead teams and coalitions of people from their own and differing cultures.

We concluded that these skills manifest themselves in various disciplines as well as general education. Thus, each major course of study at Cascadia needed to consider how to strengthen student learning in the basic skills areas identified by the SCANS report. The skills of the global worker, such as the ability to work in teams of people and with varied cultures, are relevant not only to the work environment but also to the social and political fabric of the nation. When rethinking the curriculum, we wanted these key skills manifest in both the general education course work and that specific to the major.

Students' ability to synthesize information emerged in our planning as a particularly important skill. A by-product of the information explosion is the inevitable increasing importance for learners to synthesize vast amounts of information in a meaningful way (Davis, 1995; Dolence and Norris, 1995). This skill is crucial to success in contemporary organizations and thereby needed to occupy a central place in the learning environment and educational programs at Cascadia.

The Common Core of Learning Outcomes. The college learning outcomes are goals not just for all Cascadia students but also for faculty, administrators, and staff. They are intended as an interrelated set to be practiced as lifelong learning habits. They are designed to encourage personal growth, enhance productive citizenship, and foster individual and cooperative learning. They are a basis for assessment inside and outside the classroom and among students, faculty, and staff; they guide learning, decision making, and actions by all members of the college community. They are embedded throughout Cascadia's curriculum, and students are assessed on their achievement as well as on course- and program-specific content and skills. Progress in the achievement of these outcomes is also present in the evaluation processes for administrators and staff and is part of the tenure process and evaluation of the faculty.

The Common Core of Learning Outcomes can be summarized as follows (the full Learning Outcomes Model can be viewed at http://www.cascadia.ctc.edu/LearningForTheFuture/learningoutcomes.asp):

To think critically, creatively and reflectively. Reason and imagination are fundamental to problem solving and critical examination of ideas.

To learn actively. Learning is a personal interactive process that results in greater expertise and more comprehensive understanding of the world.

To communicate with clarity and originality. The ability to exchange ideas and information is essential to personal growth, productive work and societal vitality.

To interact in diverse and complex environments. Successful negotiation through our interdependent global society requires knowledge and awareness of staff and others, as well as enhanced interaction skills.

How Learning Should Occur. The focus of CLDT and the administrative team deliberations then shifted to research on student learning styles, multiple intelligences, and developmental issues related to age, gender, race, nationality, and life experiences of the students. We turned to research on student learning, searching for models that emphasized student productivity rather than faculty productivity, characterized what students needed to learn developmentally rather than how learning could be organized by conventional disciplinary divisions, and examined student learning styles rather than faculty instructional strategies (American Association of Community and Junior Colleges, 1988; Association of Governing Boards of Universities and Colleges, 1996; Angelo, 1993; Astin, 1993; Barr and Tagg, 1995; Carter and Alfred, 1996; Chickering and Gamson, 1991; Katz and Henry, 1988; Norman, 1993; O'Banion, 1995; O'Banion, 1996; Weinstein, 1996).

Chickering and Gamson, in *Seven Principles for Good Practices in Undergraduate Education* (1991), conclude that good curricular and instructional practices (1) encourage student-faculty contact, (2) encourage cooperation among students, (3) encourage active learning, (4) give prompt feedback to students, (5) emphasize the time on task required to master the learning, (6) communicate high expectations of student and staff, and (7) respect the diverse talents and ways of learning. The primary learning environment for undergraduate students, the lecture-discussion format, can be enhanced or replaced with practices based on these seven principles. As a new institution with new curricula, Cascadia did not have to break with old habits or discard time-worn instructional techniques. Nevertheless, we needed to identify and establish the instructional practices and the curricular designs that built on the seven principles if they were to become part of the programs and courses of study offered. This was our challenge; we believe it is clearly one of the principal challenges for all institutions of the new millennium. We need to focus not so much on how faculty teach but on how students learn, thus engaging in an active educational agenda to enhance such learning (Newmann, 1993).

Strategies for Effective Learning. Some early educational research (Angelo, 1993; Astin, 1993; Bok, 1986; Chickering and Gamson, 1991; Gates, 1996; Magolda, 1996; Newmann, 1993; Norman, 1993; Pascarella and Terenzini, 1991; Weinstein, 1996) was aggregated and summarized; student learning at the undergraduate level was defined around four primary learning strategies: (1) accumulation of information and knowledge, (2) skill development, (3) conceptual development, and (4) synthesis of knowledge. We also looked at the research conducted at the Institute for Research on Learning (Institute for Research on Learning, 1997) that challenged past assumptions regarding the basic principles of effective learning. The IRL identified seven characteristics of learning that we used in designing Cascadia's new curricula: (1) learning is fundamentally social, (2) knowledge is generated in the life of communities, (3) learning is an act of membership, (4) knowing depends on engagement and practice, (5) engagement is inseparable from empowerment, (6) failure to learn is the result of exclusion from participation, and (7) we already have a society of lifelong learners. The CLDT therefore grouped courses that could be offered in learning modules to encourage collaborative learning and, where appropriate, provided simulations of specific social and cultural environments.

Today's students are attuned to working with computer-generated environments, whether by playing games, surfing the Internet, or working with interactive television systems. Research has indicated that information can be learned through a variety of media, including electronic sources, individual or group interactions with faculty, lecture-discussions, or real-life experiences, simulations, or peer study (Davis, 1995; Dolence and Norris, 1995; Gates, 1996; Gilbert, 1996; Guskin, 1995; Johnstone and Krauth, 1996; Newmann, 1993). The CLDT therefore added the use of interactive technologies and simulated laboratories as prevalent instructional strategies in Cascadia's curricular designs.

Conceptual learning takes place when students are motivated to examine and go beyond their current assumptions. It follows that successful teaching occurs when students are enticed and motivated by the excitement and interest generated in the topic and when they are given the proper tools to reflect, explore, compare, integrate, and form the proper conceptual structures. The challenge is to motivate students so that they want to do the hard work necessary for self-reflection and development. Students who are highly motivated learn more deeply and thoroughly than those who are uninterested, regardless of the instructional strategies used (Norman, 1993; Institute for Research on Learning, 1997).

Current and future generations may enter college exhibiting less ability to sustain the level of interest and attention required for deep learning. Yet these students often become highly motivated and learn quickly through interactive games, television, and films. Norman (1993) observed that game makers and entertainers knew how to capture interest and stimulate real learning in these students (albeit, learning skills and subjects largely irrelevant to higher education). He advocated merging the skills of the game maker and electronic entertainer with the educator's skills of promoting reflection and in-depth analysis.

To effect this merger and to promote active learning, new roles for faculty and new strategies for teaching are needed. Alexander Astin (1993) has identified good practices that lead to active learning in college. Teachers need to spend more time engaged in activities associated with the promotion of active student learning. These include direct individual faculty-student interaction outside the classroom and intense small group discussions inside. Faculty need to engage more in the mentoring and advising of students and in encouraging students to be involved in activities associated with success: peer-group, team-oriented learning; peer tutoring and coaching; and experiential learning outside the institution. Within this context, we envisioned new roles for Cascadia faculty as facilitators, knowledge navigators, and learner-service intermediaries (American Association of Community and Junior Colleges, 1988; Barr and Tagg, 1995; Bowen, 1992; Carter and Alfred, 1996; Davis, 1995; Dolence and Norris, 1995; Harlacher and Gollattscheck, 1996; Katz and Henry, 1988; O'Banion 1995, 1996; Rifkin, 1995, 1996; Stewart, 1996; Weinstein, 1996).

At Cascadia Community College, we sought to create a learning environment built on the findings and recommendations of Norman (1993), Chickering and Gamson (1991), Pascarella and Terenzini (1991), and Astin (1993).

From Mission to Goals and Degrees

When designing a general education curriculum (or the curriculum of an entire college for that matter), where do you begin? How do you apply the research and best practices to the design process? How do you build a general education curriculum that is meaningful, active, and engaging for students and meets the skill needs for a twenty-first-century global workforce? How do you create a curriculum that prepares students who wish to transfer and complete baccalaureate degrees at a variety of institutions, particularly the one with which we were to share a campus? Our challenge was to be both sufficiently innovative to meet student needs and employer expectations and yet adequately traditional to fit the mold of the existing general education and academic transfer practices.

Translating the Mission. We chose to begin our work by translating the key words in the college's mission into practical guiding principles for curriculum design. From our mission came our purposes for general education.

The Cascadia mission called for a "comprehensive" community college wherein general education served both students preparing to enter the workforce as well as those planning to transfer to a baccalaureate-granting institution. The general education program would also need to be fully articulated with developmental courses serving underprepared students.

The Cascadia mission demanded that the programs and services be "culturally rich." In the courses and modules created, students, faculty, staff, and the community would need to find their cultures valued and celebrated. Learning would be rich in that everyone would be encouraged to share and learn from one another in order to build a stronger society committed to work for the good of each and of all. For general education, this also meant creating a global curriculum, giving specific attention to cultures and languages of the world. The Cascadia mission required "technologically advanced" programs and services. The college district encompasses the high-technology corridor of Washington State and therefore needed to equip all students to be adept and able in the information age. Therefore, general education courses, as with all other curricular offerings, would have a high-technology component, and the college would rely heavily on technology to provide for its own learning and growth as well. Cost-effective technologies would be used to connect students to faculty and staff and worldwide resources and to enhance learner achievement. We used "learner centered" in this context to mean all members of the college community, including students, faculty, staff, and administrators.

The Cascadia mission asserted that programs should promote "high student achievement." The CLDT decided that successful progression of all students to their educational goals would be sustained in a variety of ways. First, high expectations for student achievement and success would be represented in Cascadia's learning model (communicated to the entire campus community on the college's Web site). Student success and progress through the curriculum would be reinforced through effective advising. Everywhere we tried to stress that learning comes first and the assessment of student learning is continuous. Student learning outcomes would be communicated collegewide as well. Students would be assessed and provided feedback on their achievement of content knowledge and key skills. Electronic student portfolios would be established to track student achievement. General education modules would link courses and foster collaborative learning. Peers were used wherever possible to enhance the teaching-learning process. Learning communities and courses linked by thematic strands were designed to make learning more relevant and help students place individual courses within the larger context and agenda for learning. For students who would join us on this journey of high achievement, we offered a degree completion guarantee as well.

The Cascadia mission called for "student achievement and educational excellence." We recognized that this had come to mean different things to different people, so we chose to focus on what research had shown to be the hallmarks of student success. Thus, educational excellence for Cascadia's programs was defined as having clearly defined educational outcomes; high and relevant standards for their achievement; superior instructional strategies and educational activities by which students could achieve the standards; efficient and effective use of the student's investment of time, money, and effort and the public's investment of resources in accomplishing educational aims; the vigilant application of best practices in all educational programs; and the acceptance of change as a necessary condition of a learning organization.

Cascadia's mission called for the total college curriculum to be "seamlessly linked with the community, area enterprise and educational partners." For general education, this meant ongoing assessment of courses and modules relative to employer needs for a skilled workforce, student interests and abilities, and the expectations of those public and private institutions receiving Cascadia transfer students, particularly the University of Washington, Bothell. It also called for close communication, partnership, and articulation of school reforms in the area's secondary schools. Finally, it meant that Cascadia's leadership, faculty, and staff needed to be willing to change and to be responsive to needs as they became apparent through the college's assessment processes.

General education course objectives and student outcomes were designed to meet or exceed the expectations of transfer institutions. Technical and professional degrees, including their general education components and performance standards, were validated by the businesses and industries that would employ Cascadia's graduates. Courses and modules were developed with an eye to providing practical applications of what was being learned, not only in class assignments and projects but also in career-relevant internships and service-learning opportunities. Rather than develop a course for every subject and skill we wished to convey in the new curriculum, the CLDT sought to embed key values and abilities in most all courses: respect, tolerance, and civility toward others; interpersonal skills and teamwork; collaboration, compromise, and consensus-building skills; a sense of responsibility for self and others; and honesty and integrity.

The Cascadia Learner Profile. Our next step was to create the Cascadia learner profile, a needs assessment of the educational needs of the region that described who the college's future students would be. This research resulted in a profile of learners reflective of a wide variety of needs and goals. Although it was conducted in and unique to Cascadia's district, it was also typical of many other American community colleges. The specific academic, professional, and technical programs were designed to meet the variety of needs identified. In addition, all learners, regardless of their intent, needed to master a common core of learning outcomes. Thus, creating the learner profile affirmed the need for and further specified the substance of the general education program.

Because the curriculum was developed prior to any full-time student enrollment, it was necessary to estimate the mix of students to be served. As general education in most community colleges has several masters, such planning was essential. Based on broad community input and research, as well as the colocation with the University of Washington, Bothell, the initial academic and professional and technical offerings at Cascadia were designed to fit a profile of 68 percent academic transfer students, 20 percent professional and technical students, including diploma (six-month) and certificate (one-year) programs, and 12 percent precollege, underprepared, and special needs students. This became the Cascadia learner profile from which the CLDT worked to design the curriculum. The result of this work became our current offerings of three transfer degrees, three applied degrees, and six certificate programs, most served in part by general education courses and modules.

Creating Cascadia's Curriculum

Following the analysis of the implication of Cascadia's mission for the new curriculum and after we created the Cascadia Learner Profile, we began to design the new curriculum.

Curricular Guiding Principles. The construction of the curriculum was based on principles derived from the mission, the review of research and good practices, the Cascadia learner profile, and the college's learning outcomes. These principles under which we operated were as follows: diversity and respect for difference are hallmarks of a true learning community; all members of the community are learners and must strive to make learning relevant and connected; learning is transformative and personal, and it cannot be predicted or controlled; and access is a critical factor in all decision making. These principles were next employed in the design of specific courses.

The Course Design Process. Drawing on these principles, the learner profile, and the Common Core of Learning Outcomes, the curriculum was designed, starting with the progression of course-by-course development and moving toward program and degree completion. A primary concern was to make courses relevant to students, focusing on student learning and not teaching. The following steps were followed in developing individual courses and modules:

1. Evaluate the context. Look at the broad surrounding environment, such as other schools, colleges and universities, businesses, and the community. Develop the courses and programs to meet those needs and demands.
2. Define the learning outcomes. Decide what students should know and do for that course or series of courses, programs, or degrees. Focus on student learning.
3. Describe the outcome measures. Design means by which students will demonstrate evidence of achievement of the outcomes.
4. Decide on the content. Decide what knowledge and skills need to be taught in order for students to achieve the outcomes identified in step 2.
5. Identify best practices. Choose how the course or series of courses, programs, and degrees should be presented, selecting the best possible delivery modes.
6. Return to step 1 and reassess currency and relevance.

Using this design sequence, the CLDT guided the development and implementation of courses and modules throughout the College.

General Education Requirements. The associate degrees and general education requirements at Cascadia require completion of twenty-three credits in Foundations for College Success, which encompass the areas of communication skills (college composition, writing from research and multicultural communications), college success (college success strategies, study at Cascadia, e-portfolio development and effective study techniques), and quantitative reasoning (mathematics). In addition, students must complete a cultural knowledge requirement, which can be completed through distribution requirements of humanities (fifteen credits), natural sciences (fifteen credits), social sciences (fifteen credits), and electives (twenty-two credits). Although these requirements addressed the statewide articulation and transfer policies, Cascadia adopted several features that were distinctive and that reflected its commitment to be a learning college:

- Teamwork embedded in the curriculum. Cascadia believes strongly that all students need to develop the ability to work effectively in small group settings. Teamwork directly furthers the core learning outcomes. This belief is supported by extensive research on effective teaching and learning. Employers consistently indicate that the abilities to communicate, solve problems, make decisions, and interact with diverse individuals and viewpoints in a group setting are critical to success in the workplace, no matter what type of position one holds. Students need to know how to work and interact collaboratively in order to survive in today's complex, interdependent, and increasingly international world. This is why teamwork is important to Cascadia. Students find that courses throughout Cascadia's curriculum—foundation classes, academic classes, technology classes—require them to work in group settings.

- Mathematics modules. In Cascadia's mathematics courses, students learn concepts, skills, and how math is used in life, the workplace, and other college subjects. Many math courses require students to register simultaneously in a core class and one of several modules that require the application of mathematics to the arts and sciences or to technology.

- Learning communities. Learning communities offer an alternative to the traditional individual course approach. They are courses and modules linked by specific themes and intended to ask students to synthesize knowledge and ideas across disciplines, help students understand patterns in the organization of knowledge, make connections among different fields of knowledge, and integrate their studies with personal experience and intellectual growth. A typical learning community may meet two days a week for four hours daily. It may include workshops, seminars, lectures, field trips, group projects, and writing assignments. Seminars play a crucial role in synthesizing the learning process; participants often learn to analyze and critique arguments, cooperate in group discussion, read critically, and debate logically. Writing assignments and group projects allow students to clarify and express their ideas and make connections among many subjects.

Learning communities represent an integrated educational approach to general education and to major academic and professional fields. College-level learning community courses apply to the associate of integrated studies and associate of science degrees and may transfer to other colleges and universities.

Guaranteed Associate of Integrated Studies. One unique alternative in general education at Cascadia is the guaranteed associate of integrated studies (AIS) degree. For first-generation students who may have no direct familiarity with college success and for working adults trying to balance job, family, and schooling, the AIS degree combines the basic components of student success at Cascadia. Students are guaranteed blocks of classes every quarter, enabling a sequential progress toward degree completion. They encounter the best in our educational practices, integrating knowledge skills across academic disciplines in team-taught learning communities. The organization of courses and modules into blocks provides efficiency and convenience of time as well. They know they will get the courses and sequences necessary to complete the degree. The AIS degree offers another important dimension as well. At Cascadia, we believe that integrating knowledge and skills across academic disciplines is important to becoming an educated person. This is why we offer the AIS degree as an option under the statewide direct transfer agreement.

Electronic Portfolio. At Cascadia, students develop personalized, electronic, Web-based portfolios to demonstrate their learning. The e-Portfolio provides a place to record and store a wide range of important materials and information, including career and educational goals, academic accomplishments, special projects, personal reflections, and affirmations from others. It holds tangible products that demonstrate students' skills and showcases their accomplishments. Students create an initial portfolio as part of the College Strategies or Careers in Information Technology classes and continue to add to its content throughout their college experience. The e-Portfolio is an effective way for students to demonstrate their knowledge, skills, and abilities to prospective employers or universities.

Advisory Committees and the Review of Curriculum. The CLDT and the Cascadia administrative team assembled curricular advisory committees for general education and the professional and technical programs as well. These committees were composed of faculty from neighboring community colleges, the University of Washington, Bothell, the University of Washington, Seattle, the local school districts, Evergreen State College, the Washington Center for Undergraduate Education, and Oregon State University. Each committee also had representation from business and industry and local and state governmental agencies. The advisory committees reviewed and suggested refinements to the courses. Once the courses met the design and curricular standards of the college and had received favorable reviews from the appropriate advisory committee, they became part of the self-study documentation for accreditation candidacy and state approval. Each course, program, and degree created in this way was presented for approval to the Shoreline Community College Curriculum Committee, the State Board for Community and Technical Colleges, and the State of Washington's Higher Education Coordinating Board.

Lessons Learned

It is not easy being different and innovative while at the same time fitting the mold of statewide general education standards and articulation agreements. We continue to struggle with how we present ourselves to our students and our partner institutions. Hoping to assist multiple audiences, our schedule of classes and catalogue illustrate prominently the college learning outcomes and their definitions, as well as Cascadia's learning model. In addition, this information is notably displayed in college publications.

I am pleased to report that students are thriving in the environment we have created. They are blossoming in classrooms where faculty assist them in discovering knowledge and skills and where they are expected to contribute to class by working in teams, to present their discoveries through the electronic podiums, to lead and teach others, and to be responsible for their own learning. Students have taken their learning to heights that have challenged faculty, staff, and administration and have exceeded all our expectations. We have indeed created a learning college, where all of us continue to grow and learn from ourselves and, most important, from our students.

Our best-laid plans, like those of others, needed refinement when confronted with the reality and the expectations of our students. We have entirely revised the College Strategies courses in response to requests by students as well as the faculty who have been teaching them. The e-Portfolio, which is introduced in these classes, has been improved through the input of faculty and students. We have reached a workable compromise with our university transfer partners regarding the mathematics modules and how to best translate them in order to make them transferable. We are now developing additional courses. Overall, the general education program is working very well and is well received and appreciated by students. As it grows, we continue to focus on students' strengths and build on those.

Since our belief systems and educational delivery methodologies are somewhat out of the norm, we have established two initiatives to assist us as we grow. We have launched the Employee Learning Institute to assist all employees with their personal and professional goals and to learn the "Cascadia way" by sharing our research, practices, beliefs, and organizational principles and structures. We have also established the Teaching and Learning Academy (TLA) designed primarily for the faculty to foster innovation and continuous teaching and learning improvement and a community of Cascadia scholars. Through the TLA, faculty can share experiences and grow while at the same time keeping current in the best practices.

Supporting associate (part-time) faculty is one of the central responsibilities of the TLA. Our intent is to ensure that their teaching style is learner and learning focused and that they are able to incorporate the collegewide learning outcomes into their classes. These efforts alone, however, are not sufficient, and without additional funds to support their formal participation in the TLA, maintaining a core of well-trained associate faculty will be difficult as enrollment grows.

Innovation has not trumped convention, however, and students, staff, faculty, and administrative leaders come to us from more traditional educational environments. We continue to struggle over how to best translate "seat time" requirements into "outcomes" language, searching for consistency between course outcomes, program outcomes, collegewide outcomes, and distribution area outcomes.

Finally, while we have established the e-Portfolios for students, we have just begun the work on a thorough assessment of all programs and practices. This is ongoing work as we search, learn, and apply our discoveries and continue to assess, improve, and learn. The next challenge is to create a true learning organization, one based on a culture that values its own assessment and improvement.

Next Steps: Creating a Culture of Assessment

The Cascadia faculty is organized into interdisciplinary learning outcome teams (LOTs), reflective of the four college learning outcomes. In addition each college employee—faculty, staff, and administration—and students join one of the four LOTs to participate in collegewide governance activities. The LOTs serve two functions. First, they have institutionwide responsibilities for the research, development, and assessment activities around their particular learning outcome; institutionwide communication relative to that learning outcome; and strategic planning. In this first function, LOT facilitators, appointed by and reporting to the president, lead the groups; the facilitators are employees given either a one-third release from their regular assignments or funding for support. The second function of the LOTs is focused on the conduct of teaching and learning, curriculum design and development, creation of the schedule of classes, hiring and evaluation of associate faculty, and facilitation of the tenure process, again relative to the specified learning outcome. In carrying out this second function, LOT teaching and learning leaders guide the LOTs; they are faculty on one-third release time and report to the vice president of student learning.

After spending a year in institutional-building activities, the LOTs spent the second year engaged in the creation of the rubrics for assessment of both collegewide learning outcomes and courses and programs. During the third year, the LOTs have focused on strategic planning initiatives. In addition, the college assessment team has focused on unpacking the learning outcomes and course and program outcomes, creating distinct measurable terms. An assessment fair is now in planning for the end of each quarter, where students and employees can present their achievements. Finally, the Institutional Effectiveness Committee is developing the college's learning and educational assessment plan. We are well under way, but much remains to be done.

It is said that after completing the Sistine Chapel, Michelangelo said, "*Ancora Imaparo*" (I am still learning). At Cascadia, we will always continue to learn.

References

American Association of Community and Junior Colleges. *Building Communities: A Vision for a New Century*. Washington, D.C.: American Association of Community and Junior Colleges, 1988.

Angelo, T. A. "A Teacher's Dozen—Fourteen General Research-Based Principles for Improving Higher Learning." *AAHE Bulletin*, 1993, *45*(3), 3–7, 13.

Association of Governing Boards of Universities and Colleges. *Ten Policy Issues for Higher Education*. Washington, D.C.: Association of Governing Boards of Universities and Colleges, 1996.

Astin, A. *What Matters in College? Four Critical Years Revisited*. San Francisco: Jossey-Bass, 1993.

Barr, R., and Tagg, J. "From Teaching to Learning: A New Paradigm for Undergraduate Education." *Change*, 1995, *27*(6), 12–25, 1995.

Bok, D. *Higher Learning*. Cambridge, Mass.: Harvard University Press, 1986.

Bowen, R. C. *Infusing Technology into Education*. New York: LaGuardia Community College, 1992. (ED 345 759)

Burke, W. *Organizational Development: A Process of Learning and Changing*. (2nd ed.) Reading, Mass.: Addison-Wesley, 1994.

Carter, P., and Alfred, R. L. "Transforming Community Colleges to Compete with the Future." *Journal of Academic Leadership*, 1996, *3*(3), 3–7.

Case, J. *Open-Book Management: The Coming Business Revolution*. New York: HarperCollins, 1995.

Chickering, A., and Gamson, Z. *Seven Principles for Good Practice in Undergraduate Education*. San Francisco: Jossey-Bass, 1991.

Davis, J. R. "Reengineering Teaching for Twenty-First-Century Learning." *Educational Record*, 1995, *76*, 16–22.

Dilworth, M. E., and Robinson, S. "K-12 and Postsecondary Education: Same Issues, Same Consequences." *Educational Record*, 1995, *76*(2–3), 82–89.

Dolence, M. G., and Norris, D. M. *Transforming Higher Education: A Vision for Learning in the Twenty-First Century*. Ann Arbor, Mich.: Society for College and University Planning, 1995.

Freiberg, K., and Freiberg, J. *Nuts! Southwest Airlines' Crazy Recipe for Business and Personal Success*. Austin, Tex.: Bard Press, 1996.

Garland, M., and Treisman, U. "The Mathematics Workshop Model." *Journal of Developmental Education*, 1993, *16*(3), 14–16, 18, 20, 22.

Gates, B. "Linked up for Learning." *Educational Record*, 1996, *66*(4), 34–41.

Gilbert, S. W. "Making the Most of a Slow Revolution." *Change*, 1996, *28*(2), 10–23.

Guskin, A. E. *Reducing Student Costs and Enhancing Student Learning*. Washington, D.C.: Association of Governing Boards of Universities and Colleges, 1995.

Hammer, M., and Champy, J. *Reengineering the Corporation*. New York: HarperCollins, 1993.

Harlacher, E. L., and Gollattscheck, J. F. *Leading the Way to Community Revitalization.* Washington, D.C.: American Association of Community and Junior Colleges, 1996. Institute for Research on Learning, "Seven Basic Principles for Learning." [http:/www.irl.org]. 1997.

Johnstone, S. M., and Krauth, B. "Balancing Equity and Access: Some Principles of Good Practice for the Virtual University." *Change,* 1996, *28*(2), 38–41.

Katz, J., and Henry, M. *Turning Professors into Teachers: A New Approach to Faculty Development and Student Learning.* New York: Macmillan, 1988.

Magolda, M.B.B. "Cognitive Learning and Personal Development—A False Dichotomy." *About Campus,* 1996, *1*(3), 16–21.

McIntyre, C. "Trends of Importance to California Community Colleges." Sacramento: Board of Governors, California Community Colleges, 1996. (ED 401 956)

Newmann, F. M. "Beyond Common Sense in Educational Restructuring: The Issues of Content and Linkage." *Educational Researcher,* 1993, *22*(2), 4–13.

Norman, D. *Things That Make Us Smart: Defending the Human Attributes in the Age of the Machine.* Reading, Mass.: Addison-Wesley, 1993.

O'Banion, T. "Community Colleges Lead a Learning Revolution." *Educational Record,* 1995, *76*(4), 23–27.

O'Banion, T. "Gladly Would He Learn." *On the Horizon,* 1996, *4*(1), 1, 2–5.

Pascarella, E. T., and Terenzini, P. T. *How College Affects Students: Findings and Insights from Twenty Years of Research.* San Francisco: Jossey-Bass, 1991.

Richart, M. V. "Virtual Center for Community College Transformation: A Resource Web Site and Central Depository of Transformation Initiatives." [http:/www.cascadia.ctc.edu/]. 1998.

Rifkin, J. *The End of Work: The Decline of the Global Labor Force and the Dawn of the Post-Market Era.* New York: Tarcher/Putnam, 1995.

Rifkin, J. "Preparing the Next Generation of Students for the Civil Society." *Community College Journal,* 1996, *66*(5), 20–21.

Rowley, D. J., Lujan, H. D., and Dolence, M. G. *Strategic Change in Colleges and Universities.* San Francisco: Jossey-Bass, 1997.

Simsek, H., and Louis, K. S. "Organizational Change as Paradigm Shift: Analysis of the Change Process in a Large, Public University." *Journal of Higher Education,* 1994, *65*(6), 670–95.

Stewart, T. A. "The Invisible Key to Success." *Fortune,* Aug. 1996, pp. 173–175.

Stiehl, R., and Lewchuk, L. *The Outcomes Primer: Reconstructing the College Curriculum.* Corvallis, Ore.: Learning Organization, 2000.

Treisman, P. U. *Teaching Growth and Effectiveness: An Issues Paper.* Washington, D.C.: Mathematics Science Education Board, 1994. (ED 393 673)

U.S. Department of Labor. Secretary's Commission on Achieving Necessary Skills. *What Work Requires of Schools: A SCANS Report for America 2000.* Washington, D.C.: U.S. Government Printing Office, 1991.

Washington Higher Education Coordinating Board. *Design for the Twenty-First Century: Expanding Higher Education Opportunity in Washington.* Olympia, Wash.: Washington Higher Education Coordinating Board, 1990. (ED 358 768)

Weinstein, C. E. "Learning How to Learn: An Essential Skill for the Twenty-First Century." *Educational Record,* 1996, *77,* 49–52.

Weisbord, M. R. *Discovering Common Ground.* San Francisco: Berrett-Koehler, 1992.

Zemsky, R. "To Dance with Change." *Policy Perspectives,* 1994, *5*(3), 1A–12A.

VICTORIA MUÑOZ RICHART *is the president of Cascadia Community College in Bothell, Washington.*

5

Ownership and articulation of general education can transform an institution.

The Hamline Plan: Mentoring, Modeling, and Monitoring the Practical Liberal Arts

F. Garvin Davenport

General education is the most important service we provide undergraduate students. It is an ongoing adventure of discovery, adaptation, and challenge. When any part of an undergraduate institution's curriculum—general education or the major—becomes mere routine, devoid of surprise, argument, and resistance, it is dead and ready to be replaced.

In the fall of 1984, I was returning from a year's sabbatical leave as a professor of American literature at Hamline University. Hamline is a comprehensive university affiliated with the United Methodist Church located in Saint Paul, Minnesota, offering liberal arts, education, law, public administration, and other professional fields to over three thousand students. The new dean, Jerry G. Gaff, asked me to join a curriculum task force already a year into its work of revising the general education program. I soon became involved heavily in and committed to the project, its philosophy, its politics, and its integration into Hamline's mission. Sixteen years later, as a new century begins to take shape, I am still involved in the project and its ongoing relationship to Hamline's mission.

Many saw the general education distribution requirement then in place as out of date and ready for replacement. It was a year of freshman English and a "two-of-everything" course distribution among the four disciplinary divisions. For students and faculty alike, general education was a set of requirements to get out of the way with relative ease and very little, if any, coordination. Most courses in most departments, especially introductory and lower-division courses, counted toward the distribution credit requirements.

NEW DIRECTIONS FOR HIGHER EDUCATION, no. 125, Spring 2004 © Wiley Periodicals, Inc.

While university leaders and publications made broad generalizations about the value and virtue of liberal arts, student learning outcomes were assumed but not identified, uniformly articulated, or measured.

The articulation of purpose is a vital key to any successful curriculum. For example, a colleague in Hamline's French program told of a senior advisee who felt at a disadvantage in job interviews because very few employers in the upper Midwest had need of someone with fluency in French. As this colleague's conversation with her anxious student continued, she found herself giving voice to ideas that even she herself, as a faculty member, had never fully realized or articulated. A French major knows how to read and analyze documents carefully, knows how to work in groups and share expertise, and knows how to write clearly and think on his or her feet. Did her advisee not realize all of that? "No," the student responded. "Nobody has ever told me any of those things." Not only were the purposes of general education opaque, but its integral relation with the major was ill understood and often went unexplained.

Those purposes and connections not articulated in the college years had become more transparent with time and distance. The curriculum task force discovered this as part of their work. As they began their deliberations in 1983–84, task force members interviewed Hamline alumni already launched in careers, asking what these graduates still found valuable from their college years. The alumni did not remember much about content knowledge, but they were very much aware that skills such as writing, oral presentations, and analytical thinking that they had picked up in one or several courses had served them well in their professions and careers.

Envisioning the Practical Liberal Arts

From these interviews was born in the task force's working vocabulary the phrase "practical liberal arts" and the vision of a plan that would connect the values and skills associated with the liberal arts with the needs of the various professions and careers into which students might enter over their lifetimes. The "plan" became the Hamline Plan, and the "practicality" of the liberal arts, while politically contentious in some quarters, became and has remained a major guide in Hamline's ongoing educational endeavor.

At the core of the Hamline Plan were a faculty-administered and faculty-taught full-credit first-year seminar program, a mandate that all majors offer writing-intensive courses, and a requirement that all students take at least one such writing-intensive course in each of their four years.

While many colleges have extended the scope of writing from a single composition course to a cross-curricular effort to develop writing, few parallels existed for speech. The Hamline Plan called for a speaking-across-the-curriculum requirement and was one of the earliest ventures in this skill area. Similarly, although computing was in its infancy as an intricate part of higher education, the plan incorporated understanding the computer as a tool of learning as yet another requirement.

The disciplinary breadth requirement had as its goal student understanding of "the methods of the various academic disciplines and the way in which the different areas of knowledge interact." The cultural breadth requirement was to ensure that students would gain "an awareness of the experiences and contributions of women, members of racial and ethnic minorities and people who differ in ability, age, class and sexual orientation." The LEAD requirement (Leadership Education and Development) instituted internships, work issue "seminars in connection with internships and the infusion of work-related experiences into regular curricular offerings." The purpose of the major was declared to give students a sense of depth in at least one area of knowledge and became incorporated with general education into a comprehensive plan for practical liberal learning. Although the exact wording quoted below came later, the Hamline Plan provided a major means of working toward the college's mission: "Preparing compassionate citizens of the world by helping students maximize their intellectual, creative, and leadership potential . . . connecting what we believe and what we know to what we do, in order to increase justice, opportunity and freedom for all people everywhere" (Hamline University, 2000, pp. iii, 4, 6–9).

Perhaps the most important and most controversial provision of the new curriculum was that course designations were to follow the instructor rather than the course itself. Individual instructors were asked to take personal responsibility for providing explanations as to how their course or section was to meet one or more of the Hamline Plan aims and requirements.

Governing the Reform

The plan called for the creation of a special committee, the General Education Committee (GEC), to provide academic governance and coordination to the new curriculum. The GEC members included the directors of writing, speaking, LEAD, and computing, each of whom had direct responsibility for their areas. The committee reviewed all proposals for courses to be included in the plan and worked with individual faculty members as necessary to bring proposals into line with overall curricular standards and expectations. By 1990, this work for which GEC had been originally established was thought by most to have been accomplished, and its responsibilities were returned to the Academic Policies Committee, which had overall responsibility for both general education and major courses.

In retrospect, this rather quick return of general education to a committee with numerous other duties and responsibilities was probably a mistake. Writing, speaking, LEAD, and computing had direction, but no one person was designated as responsible for directing either the cultural or disciplinary breadth portions of the curriculum.

Tensions Associated with the Reforms

From the beginning, the Hamline Plan was controversial among the faculty. Supporters pointed to the first-year seminar's goals of introducing the liberal arts and the art of learning to all new students, the plan's across-the-curriculum focus on communication and computing skills, its efforts to establish relationships among disciplines, and its overt and unapologetic focus on specific value issues of cultural breadth. The admissions staff welcomed the Hamline Plan as an outcomes-focused curriculum that was easy to distinguish from those of competitors and to communicate to prospective students and their parents. To the standard question, "What can my son or daughter do with a liberal arts education?" the answer was easy: "Here are the skills they will need in life, and here is how they will get those skills at Hamline."

Nevertheless, some academics were less convinced of the merits of the plan. Some winced at the idea of "practical" liberal arts, sensing an attack on learning for learning's sake and a surrender to vocational training and market pressure. Others, including some key supporters of the plan, worried about the ambitiousness of the changes and the faculty development resources required to make it successful. Still others thought the Hamline Plan was too complex to administer successfully or too intrusive on the instructor's control of his or her own courses. While many expressed concern about the ambitiousness of the plan, others interpreted it as yet another distribution scheme and promptly dismissed it as irrelevant to their interests and their students. Thus, a new curriculum did not alleviate opposing views among colleagues; in fact, it reinvigorated the debate.

All of us, supporters and skeptics alike, had seen from our own limited perspective a piece of the amazing creature we had brought into being. None of us in 1985 fully understood the whole elephant or the far-reaching implications of its establishment. Nevertheless, most of us began to submit course proposals to GEC, either accepting the new curriculum as a *fait accompli* or enthusiastically embracing its call for new courses and new ways of thinking about learning and teaching in general.

From Design to Execution

The required first-year seminar (FYSEM), unlike most other first-year programs, was designed as a content course that was to visibly transcend content in a deliberate focus on skills. Each faculty member was free to choose his or her own topic to use in meeting the course goals: the development of "the skills of careful reading, critical analysis, group discussion and writing," all critical aspects of college learning (Hamline University, 2000, p. 6). In short, the seminar was designed to show students "how to do college." Most departments now offer one seminar per year. Each seminar usually is rotated among departmental faculty. Topics range from AIDS to extraterrestrial life to crime and punishment to American humor and intercultural communications. Each seminar has a small budget to support social events and field trips for its members.

The professor also serves as academic adviser for the sixteen students in the seminar until they declare a major, sometimes a full year or more after the fall FYSEM. Thus, advising and general education are linked closely. More recently, a "campus colleague," or cocurricular adviser, assists seminar professors in the advising and mentoring dimension of the course. These colleagues usually are a staff member or administrator, but occasionally include a faculty member from the law school or one of the graduate programs. The FYSEM is viewed as a cooperative venture between academics and student affairs and has proven popular with the students, faculty, and "colleagues" who become involved in it.

Indeed, students often now complain that FYSEM does not continue beyond the first semester of their first year. From the outset, the seminar led to a jump in retention from first to second year. Since the second, third, and fourth semesters are also crucial to retention, we now are studying ways to continue the sense of community and "specialness" that the FYSEM creates.

The planners of the new curriculum felt confident that Hamline Plan courses would permeate the curriculum so that students could fulfill its requirements with little, if any, difficulty. Furthermore, its advocates argued that many courses could meet more than one requirement—disciplinary breadth and writing, for example, or LEAD and speaking. General education requirements could be met in introductory, intermediate, and even advanced courses across the curriculum. An advanced physics seminar that was also planned to be a writing- or speaking-intensive course, for example, would make an extremely strong statement about those skills' priorities no matter what the majors were of the students enrolled.

Courses meeting more than one general education goal or requiring a coordinated effort between teaching, advising, and mentoring necessitated a faculty prepared and motivated to accomplish these complex tasks. Because course assignments within the plan rotated among faculty members, faculty development and support needed to be broad-based and ongoing. During the early years of the plan, faculty workshops (with base-pay compensation stipends as incentives) helped faculty members better understand issues such as the pedagogical differences between requiring "lots of writing" and a "writing-intensive" course. "Writing intensive" meant that students and faculty alike were asked to focus on the revision of drafts, writing strategies, and the expectations of various audiences. While departments in the humanities and social sciences offered most cultural breadth courses, almost every department offered disciplinary breadth courses. The interest in internships and related issues began to grow. The registrar devised a process of tracking requirements that followed individual instructors rather than course numbers. Students used to the old distribution plan graduated. New students began their encounters with the Hamline Plan in the summer before their matriculation as they chose their first-year seminars. GEC continued to oversee faculty development and course approval. The new curriculum was launched and sailed forth.

Then and Now

Sixteen years later, the Hamline Plan is still a focus of discussion, still changing, and to some extent still controversial. The joys and liberating powers of learning for learning's sake have not only survived "practicality" but have flourished as preparing students for their eventual involvement in the workplace has become an increasingly important part of the overall general education program. Hamline Plan courses are spread across all departments, although never with quite as many open seats for the more popular courses as we would like. Most important, by firmly establishing the central importance of general education in a liberal arts environment, this skills-based, student-centered general educational program has provided a forum on teaching, making possible ongoing discussion and adaptation to new needs and new opportunities.

Without such a precedent and an environment that invite innovation, we would have found the going increasingly rough in the 1990s and beyond. The issues first brought to our attention by Jerry Gaff in the early 1980s and that stimulated initial work on the Hamline Plan are still with us. The ante for reform has been raised significantly, however, by issues that were just barely on the horizon in 1983, such as program assessment, ever more stringent fiscal accountability, the nature of faculty work, and the now galloping specter/opportunity of technology.

Institutional reform by definition involves compromise. It creates changes that can result in improvement, but it often does this at the cost of leaving old structures and assumptions untouched and by staying away from various sensitive issues and hard decisions. Thus, it may undermine its own chances of permanent relevance. In crafting the Hamline Plan, we had clarified our values and curricular objectives and of necessity had imposed the means by which to attain these objectives. The reforms were set on a system as old as American higher education itself—one built on departmental and disciplinary autonomy, segmented time units of courses and semesters, passive and unmonitored advising, and the primacy and sanctity of the major. General education remained campus restricted, discipline defined, course regulated, time bound, and turf governed. Education still occurred on a campus in physical spaces called classrooms and labs and was divided into segments fifty or ninety minutes long, which combined into larger units ten, fourteen, or seventeen weeks long called courses. The Hamline Plan did not challenge these conventional parameters. As a reform, it came to be applauded by all but defined and constrained by individual disciplines and too often treated a bit like the proverbial unwelcome stepchild. While students were encouraged, even expected, to put together ideas from various courses, faculty were neither trained nor inclined to model such behavior. If administrators saw the irony, they usually possessed a strong enough sense of survival to leave it alone.

What happened on Hamline's campus between 1983 and 1985 was a first encounter with this world of silos in which almost all of us had been trained. We had sensed changing needs and opportunities and had responded with imaginative curricular innovations. But institutionally, we had not committed to the gigantic and ongoing retooling—faculty development efforts in teaching and advising—that would be necessary to ensure anything approaching rapid or orderly success. We had not built in broad assessment procedures to measure change in outcomes and the general success of the skills-based program. We had not designed an articulation process that trained faculty to effectively help students understand the philosophy behind the new curriculum and how they would benefit both immediately and in the future.

Few among us had fully grasped the fact that in the future, teaching excellence would have less and less to do with professing and grading and more and more to do with mentoring, modeling, and monitoring students' success. In our collective excitement about new prospects, perhaps naively we had not yet realized that this new curricular endeavor was only the beginning of an ongoing effort to keep the liberal arts relevant and competitive as well as joyous and liberating.

Changes Going Forward

We know from all that has happened since that we were on the right path with the creation of the Hamline Plan. We better understand the magnitude of the undertaking and the commitment of resources it required. As an institution, we will remain a largely residential college based on campus, although our educational endeavors will be increasingly centered on the world.

In pursuit of our mission, we will of necessity continue to refine and expand our teaching, scholarship, and service in three areas identified directly or implicitly as part of the vision of the original Hamline Plan: interdisciplinarity and team-based problem solving, international and intercultural teaching and learning across the curriculum, and a technologically enhanced learning network made up of faculty, alumni, students, and community participants. Within this broad framework, strategic initiatives of the next five years include diversity; collaborative undergraduate research; holistic, student-centered advising and mentoring; Web-enhanced learning; and institutional outcome assessment.

We are and will be aided by many new sources of support. We have gotten a bit smarter not only about what we are trying to accomplish but how to accomplish it. Colleagues hired in the past ten years have arrived on campus increasingly well prepared for life in the liberal arts, thanks in part to the influence of projects such as the Association of American Colleges and Universities' Preparing Future Faculty, and in part to the fact that their own professional lives have been shaped by the same rapidly changing world for which we seek to prepare our students. In turn, Hamline's year-long orientation seminar for new faculty and special series of workshop luncheons for faculty teaching in the FYSEM program provide opportunities to learn institutional ropes and keep in touch with issues, objectives, and teaching strategies in undergraduate education. Hamline's membership in the Associated New American Colleges has provided a forum for the dialogue, exchange of ideas, and study of critical issues, such as the relationship between the liberal arts and the professions and the changing nature of faculty work.

In short, we seem to be reaping the benefits of a second wind in our general education efforts. Aided by an institutionwide and relatively surgical approach to strategic and budgetary planning, developmental resources in the college, including dean's grants, travel grants, and gains-sharing dollars, increasingly fund and reward groups of faculty, staff, alumni, and community colleagues willing to cross traditional lines of rank, department, discipline, and profession to pursue student-centered learning opportunities that contribute to our strategic objectives. There is no department, no field of study or performance that cannot benefit from this broad and opportunity-rich focus.

The Shape of the Second Wind of Change

Even five years ago, Hamline administrators were pleading with faculty to explore such issues and the implications for their work with students. Since then, imaginative and strategically focused proposals are coming more and more often directly from faculty. A number of faculty and faculty-staff projects and proposals already under way exemplify crossing lines and limitations in efforts to realize the Hamline vision of general education in service of its mission.

A recent Fulbright faculty scholar has developed and piloted a joint introductory course in molecular biotechnology for undergraduate science majors at Hamline and at the University of Dar es Salaam in Tanzania. Students from both schools work together by way of a WebCT software platform. The project will eventually involve exchanges of faculty and students from both schools. One of the weaknesses of our original cultural breadth requirement was that the sciences were not involved, at least in clearly articulated ways that students could easily discern and relate to their other cultural breadth experiences. The Dar es Salaam project opens that door a little wider and makes clear by explicitly modeling the connection between science and cultural breadth that general education is not excluded from the major nor can majors be concerned with technical knowledge alone. Combining our strategic interests in technologically enhanced education with our dedication to international and intercultural programs and opportunities meant to broaden understanding of various dimensions of otherness better, this project also speaks to our interests in tying the liberal arts to the professions and Hamline to the larger world community.

With support from the Ford Foundation and Hamline's Office of Academic Affairs, a faculty development seminar has investigated, discussed, and rethought interdisciplinarity in undergraduate education. Following a year of study and consultation, a group of College of Liberal Arts (CLA) faculty has restructured the international studies program. The new program, Global Studies, focuses on "a *sound general education* [emphasis added] grounded in an interdisciplinary approach, for students interested in the complex transnational political, cultural, social and economic connections and interrelationships that exist among peoples of the world" (Dusenbery, n.d., p. 1; also see Dusenbery, 2003). Although the old international studies major was touted as "interdisciplinary," it was limited mostly to cross-listed social science courses. Little attention was given to the pedagogy of interdisciplinarity itself or to the skills and abilities it imparts to students. The program now includes literature and fine arts courses. Perhaps most important, the opportunity to explore the uses of interdisciplinarity as both a teaching and learning skill are built into the major and supported by internal faculty development funding. In addition, the new program takes advantage of Web-based opportunities to link students and faculty working and thinking together across various disciplines, topics, and even geographical locations.

This newly improved program reveals both where we have been and where we are going in curricular change. Perhaps most important, it illustrates vividly that all undergraduate education—including majors and minors and even special certificates of accomplishment—is general education. At their best, all majors should mirror the values of liberal learning, particularly the belief that the exploration of knowledge is a collective pursuit. The most wonderful and useful gift we can give our undergraduate students, whatever their majors are, is the ability or skill to see and begin to understand connections and the nature of interconnectedness itself.

Not all the implications of a curricular change are immediately apparent. In our enthusiasm for establishing the original vision for the Hamline Plan, we had failed to grasp that very few of us had been trained to model what we urged our students to practice in our disciplinary breadth requirement. Under the conventional strictures of workload and role, too often reward came to faculty not for interdisciplinary exploration but for ever narrowing specialization. Interdisciplinarity as an outcome of liberal education was assumed to happen to or be mastered by students somewhere between courses or outside classrooms. To move beyond content on class time not only interfered with "coverage" but also was professionally risky. The dictum was, "As we were taught, so did we teach." I am reminded of a political science colleague who relayed that one of his mentors in graduate school strongly criticized him for quoting a novel in his dissertation. Now retired and free of disciplinary expectations, this colleague, who achieved significant recognition in the professional circles of political science, is now writing a political novel. My hope is to get him back on campus to mentor and model for students the risks and the payoffs of thinking both scientifically and artistically about the intersections, paradoxes, and contradictions of politics with the social and cultural context in which they occur.

The French program has challenged the concept of course and time line by redesigning its offering so that students progress at their own speed through the various units, even beyond the traditional drop-dead end of term, and can move between levels within the same semester depending on their progress. Most of the teaching and learning is done around tables in computer labs, with instructors working with individual students or very small groups. On-line aspects of the courses are available anywhere at any time, computer access being the only requirement. The French program has challenged some traditional notions of time and space for learning, has blurred the distinctions between the aims of the major and general education, and has given specific focus to student learning and success through these changes.

For the past year, a group of faculty and staff have been working on a plan for assessing student writing skills. Institutional assessment of specific components of the Hamline Plan has been long overdue, and this is a major step in rectifying this problem. In the fall of 2001, the summer reading for all first-year students, Jon Krakauer's *Into the Wild* (1997), served as the basis for a writing assessment pretest for all incoming first-year students. An outside reader, usually a specially trained graduate student, reads each essay, and the evaluation is shared with the student as a guide to the further development of his or her writing skills.

The writing assessment project is a first step toward a program that seeks to combine faculty development in holistic advising, mentoring, and monitoring of student program with that in the development of electronic portfolios of student assessments and accomplishments. Supported by effective faculty training, holistic faculty advising, especially in the crucial three semesters following the FYSEM semester, will focus on opportunities for specific skills development, such as internships, team problem solving, off-campus study, collaborative research, graduate school, career preparation, and national fellowships. To be effective, such a holistic system of advising, assessment, and articulation must begin even before matriculation and continue through graduation and beyond. In this manner, those who as students we advised become our advisers in helping the next generation of students prepare for lives as "compassionate world citizens."

Two major grants, one from the National Science Foundation supporting a Hamline partnership with the 3M Corporation and another from the Bush Foundation, have enhanced significantly our progress in providing professional development in support of fulfilling the Hamline Plan.

These grants created exciting and challenging new opportunities for faculty to help prepare students for the workplace while providing them with new models for college and departmental governance and problem solving.

The NSF-sponsored GOALI project (Grant Opportunities for Academic Liaisons with Industry) was patterned from a luncheon conversation several years ago convened by a senior professor in chemistry and a colleague in biology. This event brought together a cross-section of Hamline's science faculty and a dozen representatives from major Twin Cities corporations and successful start-up companies. The dialogue had one simple convening question: "What skills do you want your new employees—our graduates—to bring to your organization?" The answers from this and subsequent seminars have been unanimous, loud, and clear: graduates should possess the ability to communicate, work in teams and in different cultural contexts, and think both analytically and creatively. One corporate vice president for accounting astounded us all when he added, almost as an afterthought, "and a sense of history." This luncheon conversation both reaffirmed the perceptions and goals of the original Hamline Plan, but became the beginnings of what I refer to as our "second wind" of curricular change to demonstrate and articulate the values of a liberal arts education.

While the GOALI grant gave attention primarily to the sciences, a Bush Foundation faculty development grant, "Strengthening Undergraduate Education Liaisons with the Workplace," included departments and disciplines outside the sciences. It furthered efforts to focus on learning projects such as increasing liaisons with the workplace, developing service-learning courses and workshops, developing and expanding internships, and holding workshops to help faculty learn how to use team problem solving as both a teaching pedagogy and a means of making certain faculty duties, such as committee work, more efficient and effective. The NSF and Bush grants were important catalysts to change that dovetailed nicely with and complemented other general education initiatives at Hamline.

For example, one GOALI project team is identifying writing and speaking competencies specific to the sciences and is linking these to classroom activities mentored and modeled by science faculty. "Technical Work, Teams and Conflict" is a pilot course for majors in biology, chemistry, math, and physics team-taught by two CLA professors, neither of whom is in the sciences. The course is designed to "build basic knowledge and skills in areas that have been identified as weaknesses in scientific and technical job candidates and employees: social conflict, team work, and cultural diversity." Generally supported by science division faculty, the course meets three Hamline Plan requirements: disciplinary breadth in social science, cultural breadth, and oral communication. The course also includes four off-campus lab days designed to "immerse students in discussion and interaction with professionals and each other on the themes of [the] course" (Bell and Bonilla, 2001, p. 1).

The coordinator of the Bush grant, circulating among various departments, faculty interest groups, and team initiatives, realized that while numerous groups were involved in shaping the curricular innovations and needed changes, there was little awareness within any one group of what other groups were doing. Thus, the necessity of ongoing communication once again came to the fore and has resulted in a renewed effort to help faculty across the campus to understand programmatic and student needs and opportunities, better appreciate exciting changes under way, and feel more welcome to participate in the reforms. Communication in support of the reforms spreads through invitational lunches, open forums, on-line discussions, and occasional informal faculty chats. As CLA dean, I hold biweekly coffee hours, meetings of department chairs, and faculty retreats to enable a progressively broader base of faculty ownership in various general education projects, thereby minimizing the need for overt administrative or top-down steerage.

Nowhere has broad faculty ownership and the benefit of ongoing communication been more evident than in the cultural breadth requirement of the Hamline Plan, reflecting the belief held by most faculty that diversity broadly understood is essential to any general education program claiming to prepare its students for contemporary life and the future. Like the disciplinary breadth requirement, cultural breadth was instituted without any assessment of student learning outcomes beyond a passing grade in a particular course. There was no mechanisms to ensure that links had been made between various aspects of the topic as covered in class with those made in other classes or anything happening beyond the classroom.

The issue of cultural breadth has been supported by the tenacious dedication of a sizable group of faculty through a variety of means, including the recruitment and retention of faculty and staff of color and examining diversity-related issues of classroom pedagogy and the politics of cultural diversity on campus. Taking the name of a local Italian restaurant where some early meetings were held, the Lido Group has sought and found allies among students, key faculty committees, and CLA administrators.

The Lido Group has held that simply being in favor of a diverse, affirmative, multicultural campus is not enough. Indeed, such lip-service, combined with various forms and levels of intellectual or emotional naiveté, can be counterproductive or, worse, destructive. The group members have urged that we all come to understand our own perspective from the points of view of others and that Hamline as an institution commit time, money, and educational expertise to the development of a diverse campus of students, faculty, staff, and curriculum. This conviction became manifest in the college's 1997 five-year strategic plan in the first of three broad strategic objectives: "To establish and maintain a diverse community." Significant and specific increases in the number of students of color, the number of faculty and staff of color and international students, and the number of Hamline students studying abroad are spelled out in the revised draft of the plan currently under consideration by the Planning and Development Committee (PDC). In this sense, general education became more permeable and transparent, reflecting and institutionalizing the emergent values of the campus community.

In the fall of 2001, the PDC, with strong support and assistance from the Lido Group and other interested faculty members, arranged the annual two-day faculty conference around a broad array of diversity issues. Relying entirely on expertise from within the college, the university office of student affairs, and the graduate programs, the sessions reflected years of accumulated scholarship and classroom experience relative to diversity at Hamline. All sessions received high marks from participating faculty for both the theoretical background and hands-on practicality provided. There were sessions focused on teaching, scholarship, and service, illustrating that diversity and related issues affect each of the three traditional areas of faculty work.

Like the cultural breadth requirement, the first-year seminar program has also evolved since its inception. The one-semester course has proved to be generally popular with students, their parents, and most of the faculty who teach it. Each FYSEM instructor is strongly encouraged to choose a topic for his or her individual sections that will fulfill the FYSEM goals *and* relieve the instructors from the temptations, obligations, and limitations of "covering the topic," as that term is usually understood in curriculum development and college teaching. A colleague in the religion department, for example, teaches a FYSEM about the Civil War as a cultural phenomenon. A chemist offers hers on "Feeling Minnesotan," which considers issues of regional identity. For several years, I offered "The Mighty Mississippi," which, instead of focusing on literature, used such topics as the origins of the milling industry in the St. Anthony Falls historic district of Minneapolis and the politics and engineering of sewage treatment in the Twin Cities today. These give but a taste of the topical platform on which the FYSEM stage was constructed.

The challenges of such a course are those of a multisectioned course conducted by an interdisciplinary mix of instructors and topics. Can instructors from twenty or more departments and programs, each teaching a different topic, provide learning experiences that incorporate common goals and outcomes? Can all students enrolled in these various sections come to understand that they are in the same course regardless of section, that the bar is equally high in every section, and that the work and rewards are similar regardless of the particular topic of a particular section?

These issues of focus and quality control require constant attention. The ever rotating FYSEM faculty, with the assistant or associate dean as coordinator, has met regularly for years, very much like a department, in the spring to discuss and plan the next fall's sections and in the fall to share concerns, accomplishments, and problems in the currently offered sections. Individual sections are now offered at a common hour on either a Monday-Wednesday-Friday schedule or a Tuesday-Thursday schedule to encourage interaction between and among sections. All instructors are asked to include certain common projects or assignments. One such FYSEM activity common among sections is the major exploration assignment, in which each student does a short research project on a possible major, including interviews with faculty in the appropriate department or departments and students currently majoring in that subject.

The highlight of each fall's FYSEM program is the Fall Fair, which can most easily be described as a poster session with cotton candy. Designed as a celebration of learning and as the first in a Hamline student's development as a scholar and citizen, the fair combines interactive and sometimes highly entertaining poster presentations prepared by the students in each FYSEM along with departmental major-minor tables staffed by both faculty and students. The event is widely advertised across campus as well as to local prospective students and their families, who are special guests. The fair cuts across the campus dinner hour, guaranteeing the consumption of great quantities of pizza, soft drinks, cotton candy, and other assorted foods against the sounds of diverse music both live and recorded. The added colors of appropriately costumed presenters and performers add a carnival-like atmosphere to the more serious academic framework of the event. Students working their particular poster or exhibit become teachers. Moving from exhibit to exhibit, professors, administrators, and visitors alike become students. Most important, the FYSEM students get their first taste of sharing what they know and what they are learning with a diverse and supportive general audience.

The fair is the first event in a sequence that for many students will include an initial independent study, usually in the sophomore year, a collaborative research project with a professor during the junior or senior year, and a departmental honors project, with recognition at commencement, during the senior year. Thus, the foundational skills of close reading skills, analytical thinking, teamwork, and learning through discussion, introduced during the FYSEM, expand and intensify throughout a student's four years. As a part of the increasing emphasis on the articulation of goals and expectations and as a preview of coming attractions and possibilities, we also urge FYSEM instructors to tour with their first-year and sophomore advisees the Spring Honors Day poster sessions. Seniors who are doing more advanced collaborative research and departmental honors projects organize these sessions.

Over the past fifteen years, general education has moved from a consideration of which great books or which survey courses constitute a proper or essential liberal education toward a skill-based restructuring of both form and content across the entire curriculum. How to teach—whether to first-year students or to seniors—has become as important as what to teach. Pedagogy itself has become a legitimate field of scholarship in higher education as it has always been in the K–12 classroom. What we are learning is that teaching now and in the future is less about professing information or even interpretation of that information. Rather, it is about mentoring, modeling, and monitoring.

It is about mentoring students in their own discovery process: helping them learn that questions are more important in the educational process than answers and helping them to see that failure is sometimes the greatest aid of all to learning, but only if they get a chance to try again.

Thus, teaching is also about modeling the skills we wish students to learn by writing with our writing students, experiencing the off-campus workplace with interning students, and doing primary research with all students.

And finally, teaching is about monitoring the outcomes—measuring what students know when they come to Hamline and correcting our course as navigator teachers in accordance, taking full advantage of such new aids as the computer and reconstructed concepts of "class" and "hour" to let students learn in a way that best works for them. These lessons are not necessarily easy for any of us, especially those of us who grew up in the world of oaken lecterns, yellowed lecture notes, and final blue books. But they are lessons that are absolutely essential to learn as we consider liberal arts and general education

After all the vision statements and curricular reforms and strategic planning, I am convinced that the ongoing and enthusiastic ownership of the Hamline Plan by faculty as it is articulated to colleagues, students, and staff alike is the single most important ingredient in the success of our general education program, as it is in the success of any other liberal arts program.

This is general education for the future. Another way to say this is that the future is general education. Preparing students to master their lives in this new century means helping them from their first-year seminars through their senior seminars to master the skills of formulating questions, making connections between ways of learning as well between facts, working in culturally and professionally complex teams, and "connecting what we believe and what we know to what we do, in order to increase justice, opportunity and freedom for all people everywhere." This is the practicality of the liberal arts.

References

Bell, C., and Bonilla, J. F. "CFST 3980: Technical Work, Teams and Conflict." Unpublished course summary, 2001.

Dusenbery, V. A. Unpublished proposal for revision of the international studies major, n.d.

Dusenbery, V. A. "Constructing an Interdisciplinary Global Studies Major." *Hamline Review*, 27(3) 2003, 1–16.

Hamline University. *2000–2002 Bulletin*. St. Paul, Minn.: Hamline University, 2000.

Krakauer, J. *Into the Wild*. New York: Doubleday, 1997.

F. GARVIN DAVENPORT is dean of the college of liberal arts and professor of English at Hamline University.

Most want a more coherent curriculum. Few succeed.
What works, and why?

Creating Coherence: The Unfinished Agenda

D. Kent Johnson, James L. Ratcliff

Nearly everyone has a stake in general education. Consider all the constituents participating in general education reforms at American University; the critics claimed the prior program was an amalgamation of the political interests across campus. Because so many of the institution's stakeholders had varying perspectives and interests, tensions ensued at several levels. Tensions are the result of conflicting or divergent perspectives, including those held by a single individual with conflicting roles (departmental faculty member and member of the general education task force).

At the course and program level, tensions exist as to what to teach, how to organize the curriculum, whether classic or contemporary texts should provide focus, to what extent the needs of the individual or creation of community should prevail—to name but a few (Association of American Colleges, 1988). Another source of tension emanates from the role that general education plays in undergraduate degree programs and, in particular, its relationship to majors (see Chapter One). Although many institutions, like Franklin Pierce, are integrating general education into all four years of the baccalaureate degree, others view it as the introduction and precursor to specialization and professional socialization. A further source of tensions comes from the relationship between the academic programs of the institution and social expectations. These are expressed locally and within a state over such issues as student transfer policies, statewide general education requirements, the assessment of student learning, and the expectations that various career fields, professions, and disciplinary majors place on the general education program. These tensions are reflected in national discourse as well.

NEW DIRECTIONS FOR HIGHER EDUCATION, no. 125, Spring 2004 © Wiley Periodicals, Inc.

Curricular Tensions and General Education Reform

Between 1984 and 1993, twelve national reports appeared that were critical of undergraduate education; eight others proposed specific reforms with direct implication for general education (many were reviewed briefly in Chapter One and are described more fully in Chapter Seven). Collectively, they claimed that the baccalaureate degree had lost meaning, advocated that the curriculum should resonate more clearly with the broader collegiate experience, and called for general and liberal learning to be regarded as "the most important course of study during the undergraduate years" (Stark and Lattuca, 1997, p. 62). As we have noted elsewhere, the reports and reform proposals of the late 1980s and early 1990s set the stage for a wave of revision and reform on campuses across the country.

There continue to be substantive areas where tensions in the curriculum are likely to emerge. Newton (2001) identified four perennial dimensions of general education likely to generate tension in curricular reform:

- Unity versus fragmentation (knowledge)
- Breadth versus depth (student learning)
- Generalists versus specialists (faculty competence)
- Western culture versus cultural diversity (content)

These tensions, left unresolved, inhibit general education reform.

In addition, the CAO 2000 survey (Johnson, 2003) indicated three areas of ongoing tension leading to curricular change in general education:

- How to increase curricular coherence and meaning
- How to address changing student and faculty needs
- How to update and renew the general education program

Survey responses and anecdotal comments confirmed each as a source of ongoing tension (Johnson, 2003). The Association of American Colleges (1988), Stark and Lattuca (1997), and Newton (2001) reported similar areas of tension, suggesting they are perennial in nature. In the broadest sense, the impetus to change invites questions of what and how to teach, how to best meet individual and community needs, what the role of faculty is in delivering the curriculum, and how the curriculum is best organized to address these potentially conflicting needs. Answers to these are many and varied.

Reform of general education is often regarded as an overwhelming complex, time-consuming, and politically fractious endeavor. However, the GE 2000 survey and the cases presented in this volume show that revising the general education curriculum is not only possible but also prevalent. Conventional approaches to change often call for broad campus consensus. From this perspective, failure to resolve endemic tensions in the general education curriculum is a barrier to change (Newton, 2001). Nevertheless, the research presented here suggests that tensions are inherent in general education change and may generate new patterns of general education, embracing the notion of continuous change (as described in Chapter Seven), and consistent with the recommendations of *A New Vitality in General Education* (Association of American Colleges, 1988; Ratcliff, Johnson, La Nasa, and Gaff, 2001; Johnson, 2003).

Many of these tensions center on creating a coherent curriculum and specifically on how best to provide common meaning for students enrolled. What creates the common experience in general education? Is it that all students must experience the same courses (that is, the core)? Is it that all students must achieve the same aims (common outcomes)? Is it that students must share the same college experience regardless of major (learning communities, clusters, or something else)? What should students experience in common through general education has been asked philosophically (mission and goals), substantively (great books, core curriculum), structurally (distributional requirements, articulation agreements), and experientially (learning communities, freshman seminars). The issue of commonality begs the larger one: What makes for a coherent curriculum and a meaningful experience in general education? In this chapter, we examine these questions.

Coherence: The Elusive Element

Creating a coherent curriculum has been a primary aim of general education reforms. Noticeable in the GE 2000 and CAO 2000 surveys, however, was the lack of a consistent view of what curricular coherence is. Most saw coherence as somehow related to conveying meaning to students, faculty, or other constituents. Many institutions used their general education program to convey institutional values and mission to key constituents. As such, general education represented a key, albeit implicit, policy statement, as well as a definition of a major element of the undergraduate experience. Most leaders believed that increasing curricular coherence results in programs that more clearly articulate the knowledge and skills associated with a college education.

Many general education leaders and chief academic officers thought that their most recent rounds of general education revisions fell short of the mark in improving coherence. As has been the case in the past (Association of American Colleges, 1985; Gaff, 1991; Study Group on the Conditions of Excellence, 1984; Weingartner, 1992; Zemsky, 1989, Ratcliff, 2000), they nonetheless continued to work toward increased coherence as a principal remedy for an undergraduate degree perceived to be fragmented.

General education leaders associated reducing and tightening distribution requirements, establishing and refining core programs, and integrating courses across disciplines with creating coherence. These practices, consistent with the academic planning paradigm (Stark and Lattuca, 1997; Tyler, 1950), assumed that curricular coherence comes from faculty work in refining courses and conducting assessments that conform to preset goals. From this view, understanding results from clarity of goals and tying requirements and assessments to the goals. It requires no input or action on the part of the student, and it does not take into account student perceptions of the curriculum (except as perceived by faculty working on revisions). In short, faculties plan coherence, and as a result, students achieve integration (Stark and Lattuca, 1997).

Coherence may be better seen as also happening in the minds and discourse of students. In this sense, students make connections among ideas, assimilate them into their own conceptual frameworks, and apply them to problems and situations they care about. Faculties and the curriculum facilitate this learning process wherein knowledge, skills, and attitudes are developed. The implication of this alternate frame for coherence is that coherence is an ongoing process of reconciling tensions to facilitate complex meaning in the minds of individual students rather than an attempt to resolve tension to communicate a singular vision to all students.

Coherence may be better encouraged by bringing together competing tensions in general education. The process of curricular change involves tension between unifying (centripedal) and stratifying (centrifugal) forces. The expansion of knowledge, the subspecialization of curricula to meet the diversification of students and their abilities and interests, and the elaboration of courses to meet the social, technical, economic, and political priorities of society all serve as centrifugal forces of curricula. The search for coherence serves as a centripedal force, working to bring pieces of knowledge and representations of meaning into relationships that are understandable to learners and others. The tension between centrifugal and centripedal forces in the curriculum assumed a politicized form of "culture wars" in the 1980s: the battles among academics as to the canonization of texts within fields (Graff, 1992). One can imagine a body of knowledge, pushing itself asunder and packing itself together by the power of centrifugal and centripedal forces of debate within the academy, with these swings reflected in the general education program (Ratcliff, 2000).

The tremendous changes in the knowledge base making up the disciplines and professions, profound social and demographic changes, and increasing public scrutiny of higher education conspire to generate centrifugal forces on the curriculum. Inaction, from this vantage point, does not lead to status quo but rather to the erosion of coherence over time. Under such conditions, it is not surprising to see widespread concerted efforts to counteract these centrifugal tendencies through revisions aimed at improving coherence.

An emerging trend found in the GE 2000 and CAO 2000 surveys was using curricular themes to help students make sense of the general education program. Themes were exemplified in the Franklin Pierce and Hamline plans. Themes were thought to give students a basis for making curricular choices on the substantive focus of the theme, potentially increasing the students' involvement in making connections among courses. Similarly, themes linked courses together toward perhaps a more concrete end than the broad general education goals or a philosophy statement on the purpose of liberal learning. These trends suggested that general education leaders were moving beyond purely structural solutions to coherence, emphasizing the connectivity of curricula.

Three questions in the CAO 2002 survey help color how academic leaders are tackling the challenge of improving coherence. The first of these asked the chief academic officer (CAO) what the primary reasons were for the previous curricular revision. The second asked the CAO to describe the most notable feature of the current general education program. A third asked the CAO to look to the future and to describe the greatest challenges for general education at their institutions. Collectively, the responses to these questions portrayed how colleges were planning for greater coherence and connection in general education.

Planning for Greater Coherence

Most institutions tried to improve coherence through increasing programmatic structure. Although the total number of required credits and relative proportion of credit hours for general education did not change from 1990 to 2000, the knowledge domains required in general education expanded (see Chapter One). The modal number of credits within conventional categories, especially in the broad areas of the humanities, social sciences, and foreign language, decreased, while a wide range of particular content and skill areas was added. In this way, general education became both broader and more prescribed. Many CAOs thought that reducing choice and increasing prescription led to increased coherence.

Coherence was further tied to structuring general education to align with goals better, more effectively integrating general education with the major, and increasing the extent to which general education courses related to each other. One CAO commented, "We need to tie general education to mission; the current curriculum is out of date and does not address coherency or needs." Continuing, he described the new general education program as "a common core through four years that is interdisciplinary and team taught, includes a capstone experience and service learning." A core curriculum, within this context, is one that prescribes what the student takes, although many cores do not include interdisciplinary courses.

Core curriculums were popular solutions to curricular fragmentation in the general education literature (Bennett, 1984; Cheney, 1989; Boyer, 1987). Yet a core curriculum alone was not able to render coherence, according to the comments of one CAO: "The previous core curriculum was too disparate and lacked focus. It had weak control over what was considered a core course. It lacked obvious coherence." When the structure afforded by a core failed to produce the desired coherence, more structure was seen as the solution. This time, a common format for all core courses was the proposed solution: "Coherence is established not by blending substance and crossing disciplinary lines but by establishing a common form for all core courses." Programmatic coherence came from a common format for core courses, and coherence within the individual courses came from the disciplines offering them.

CAOs at institutions with distributional plans also gravitated toward structural solutions to coherence. Similar to the changes at American University, general education goals were reexamined and clarified in the light of institutional values, and the number of course choices afforded to each distributional category was reduced. For example, in discussing a 1997 revision to general education, one CAO commented, "The previous program had become very unwieldy. It was a distributional model with nearly 350 course options. The aims and goals of the program were vague. It had been revised piecemeal over the years." The CAO next described how general education had been changed:

> We have a much more precise set of aims and goals driving the program. There are fewer course options (approximately 95). We now have a general education capstone class, which is intended to be taken near the end of the students' gen ed experience. It is designed to serve two primary purposes: (1) to integrate the students' gen ed experiences in a writing- and discussion-intensive class, and (2) to focus on a major public affairs issue facing the USA and/or world in the next century. This latter purpose allows us to integrate our institutional mission in public affairs into the curriculum. We also have an upper-level writing class that is designed to permit students to learn how to write in their intended major.

Whether the general education program was a prescribed core or a conventional distributional requirement, the changes undertaken frequently did not result in greater coherence. While fragmentation and lack of coherence were the primary reasons for changing the general education program, only 38 percent reported that the resulting changes led to coherent sequences of courses. Although further planning and additional structure were preferred solutions, only 39 percent of GEAs reported regularly reviewing the coherence of the general education program. And although coherence was a primary reason for reform, it was not a predominant criterion for curricular reviews (Johnson, 2003).

Tackling the Sources of Incoherence

As suggested previously, coherence exists in the minds of students as well as in the creation of curricular structures (Gamson, 1989; Ratcliff, 2000). Moving attention from transmission (that is, the design and delivery of the curriculum to students) to how students receive the curriculum requires a different set of conceptual tools. First among these is to see the curriculum as a form of communication and discourse, not only from the institution to the students but among and between students, faculty, and academic leaders. As a form of communication, curriculum can be deemed incoherent if it appears irrelevant, offers too much or too little information, appears obscure or indirect, or appears inaccurate or incorrect (Ratcliff, 2000). Incoherence is in the eyes of the beholder.

One CAO described the principal strategy for bringing coherence to the curriculum as "linking courses throughout the general education curriculum by common themes. Interested faculty agree to infuse their courses with a focus on a given theme. Students with an interest in having an integrated thematic connection among several courses may take them whenever they are offered and fit into the student's schedule rather than having to try to take several in a single semester or year."

Several points are illustrated by the example. First, the students need to see the relevance of the curriculum. This was evident in the comment that course work supporting the major helped students understand the relevance of general education. Second, the CAO valued finding creative ways to maintain high student interest in the general education program. Using a thematic approach was intended to cause students to replace scheduling constraints as the primary basis for course selection. Naturally, the inherent interest of the theme to the student has direct bearing on the success of this approach.

A second source of incoherence is information overload or underload (Ratcliff, 2000). A recent graduate summarized his undergraduate experience as the required reading of hundreds of books and articles without any context beyond that provided by the individual course, resulting in the student's perceived inability to incorporate ideas into meaningful pursuits (Haworth and Conrad, 1997). The student's complaint illustrates how too much information without sufficient time and concerted energy devoted to analysis and synthesis may lead to perceived incoherence. A purpose of the seminar in the liberal arts at Franklin Pierce and many capstone seminars is to render meaning from disparate forms of knowledge, thereby reducing the prospect of information overload.

Similarly, several CAOs believed that themes not only increased the meaning to students but also promoted deeper learning and helped students to make connections between the subjects they were studying. Meaning could come from the connection between courses within the theme or between the theme and the student's major.

A third source of perceived incoherence comes from the program as being seen as too abstract or obscure. For many career-oriented students, liberal learning by and large and general education specifically do not relate immediately to their career goals and ambitions or to the role they see a college education playing in achieving those ends. The emphasis at Hamline on a practical liberal arts education and the focus on core competencies needed in the workplace as a centerpiece for the Cascadia curriculum are program characteristics intended to make general education less abstract and more accessible to students.

Another means to make general education less abstract and obscure is to tie it to the needs of the local community or region. One CAO described an institutional plan to "infuse the general education experience with themes reflecting our institutional commitments to the Appalachian region." The use of themes allowed the largely nontraditional and career-oriented student population to see liberal learning and general education as concrete manifestations of the institution's involvement in the communities and issues of the area. Also, by affording students the opportunity to integrate general education course work with regional concerns, it gave them a more holistic view of their educational experience, making it less obscure and abstract.

A fourth cause of incoherence comes from when communication is seen as inaccurate or incorrect. This often has less to do with the content and organization of the curriculum and more to do with how it is communicated. If, for example, general education is seen as a "take two of everything" requirement to "get out of the way"—to use Garvin Davenport's description of the Hamline curriculum prior to the reform—then general education has no meaning beyond the time, effort, and expense required to accumulate the necessary credits. Also, it sends the message that certain courses (those in the major) are more valuable than those in general education. Even if the catalogue states clear goals and links general education requirements to those goals, that clarity can be quickly sacrificed when faculty advisers or fellow students imply or say that the general education course work serves little purpose other than as an obstacle to entering the major or achieving graduation.

Coherence: The Unfinished Agenda

Creating coherence remains a great unfinished agenda for general education. The GE 2000 survey showed that the resultant general education designs were somewhat disconnected from a primary reason for undertaking the reforms in the first place. According to the CAOs, the perceived lack of coherence was one of the most common reasons for changing the general education curriculum. Yet at 38 percent of the institutions surveyed, coherence was not given a priority in the planning or review processes. Why is coherence not given greater attention?

That curricular coherence is often discussed in the literature but rarely formally defined may contribute to this disconnect. Another explanation may be the overwhelming reliance on the planning model implicitly used by academic leaders to create curricular change in general education. The model claims victory over fragmentation when purposes, processes, organization, and evaluation are tightly aligned. Yet the adoption of a core curriculum or the reduction of choice in a distributional plan did not lead necessarily to improved coherence in examples cited previously.

Viewing the general education curriculum as a form of oral and written communication changes the conceptualization of coherence. As new information enters each field of knowledge, as new students with new interests, backgrounds, and experiences enter the institution, and as new institutional and social priorities emerge, the general education curriculum is caught in the tensions generated by these forces and their attendant stakeholder perspectives. Collectively, these represent centrifugal forces nudging the curriculum to fragmentation, creating the impetus to add new courses and choices and necessarily leading to ever greater disarray.

Coherence appears as the result of efforts to bring together competing tensions in the curriculum. Thus, "from a relational viewpoint, efforts to achieve greater coherence can be seen as a countervailing force in a dynamic to generate meaning" (Ratcliff, 2000, p. 12). Coherence may be defined, then, as the extent to which students and faculty find meaning in the curriculum.

Classic areas of tensions in general education—unity versus fragmentation of the knowledge, breadth versus depth in student learning, generalists versus specialists in faculty preparation, staffing and development, Western culture versus cultural diversity in content—can be addressed but not conclusively resolved through curricular change. Instead, they represent dimensions of the ongoing challenges in addressing the multiple perspectives on the purpose and meaning of general education. An individual institution may adopt a general education program that answers questions of unity and fragmentation, depth and breadth, staffing and texts, but in doing so, it will not erase the multiple stakeholder perspectives and attendant relational dynamics that lead to further revision and refinement. As Garvin Davenport noted in Chapter Five, sixteen years after its initial implementation, the Hamline Plan is "still under discussion, still changing, and to some extent still controversial." Haig Mardirosian described in Chapter Three general education at American University as still a "work in progress." Such views complement and affirm those of Peter Senge (1993), who held that the impetus to change is derived from the gap between vision (what we want to create) and current reality, and this gap represents creative tensions within learning organizations. Similarly, for Jack Lindquist (1997), the "performance gap" between goals and current learning conditions was a primary driver in case studies of curricular change in the 1970s. Tensions in general education curricula stimulate rather than inhibit change. Change in general education is an ongoing process driven by the dynamics ensuing from tensions in the curriculum. (This conclusion and its implications for understanding change in general education are further explored in Chapter Seven.)

At American University, the next iteration of general education reform may be the university college. This boundary-spanning organizational structure for general education challenges the ownership of general education by conventional disciplinary departments and the integration of student learning responsibilities of academic and student affairs divisions. The impetus for this boundary spanning between academic and student life domains was the need for a "broader, cohesive, and universal plan for all its students" (Mardirosian, cited in Johnson, 2003). It also fosters ongoing need for a curriculum that is adjustable and responsive to changes in student and societal needs.

Davenport noted how dialogue among faculty and industry leaders at Hamline had presented new challenges to providing a general education program true to the "practical liberal arts." While these conversations reaffirmed the goals of the existing program, they also led to a second phase of general education renewal aimed at more clearly articulating the values of a liberal education.

The need for ongoing change, revision, and reform offers a new perspective on coherence and helps formulate an answer to the question posed at the outset of this chapter: "What creates the common experience in general education?" Commonality is not generated automatically from all students taking the same courses unless the core conveys a set of values, an intellectual perspective, or an inclination to inquiry that is seen and shared by students and faculty alike. Common goals and objectives alone do not generate coherence. Goals are things that can be kept in mind and should be the objects of genuine student effort. General education goals may appear on the syllabi of courses, but unless they are something that faculty strive to teach and students are challenged to master, they will not produce coherence. And what about those innovations, like learning communities, linked courses, and course clusters, designed to have students experience the curriculum as a cohort? Do they produce coherence? Again, our answer relates to the emblems of meaning associated with the experience. Are students and faculty alike challenged, enlightened, and engaged? Several pathways can be beat to coherence, each conveying meaning and value to general education.

General education programs need to be reviewed regularly for coherence if improvement is to be achieved. We have proposed four simple criteria that can be employed in rooting out the incoherent: (1) irrelevance, (2) information overload or underload, (3) obscure or indirect content or learning processes, and (4) incorrect or inaccurate representations of the program. Coherence is in the eye of the beholder, and it is an important, if elusive, goal. If the goal is to be achieved, greater attention needs to be given to creating coherent sequences of courses—sequences that convey the values and goals of general education to the students and faculty. Coherence is an aspiration for which an academic community must continually search. Reflection, formal assessment, and much discussion are requisite elements. This is not a simple, one-time review task but an ongoing agenda.

References

Association of American Colleges. *Integrity in the College Curriculum: A Report to the Academic Community*. Washington, D.C.: American Association of Colleges, 1985.

Association of American Colleges. *A New Vitality in General Education.* Washington, D.C.: Association of American Colleges, 1988.

Bennett, W. J. *To Reclaim a Legacy: A Report on the Humanities in Higher Education.* Washington, D.C.: National Endowment for the Humanities, 1984.

Boyer, E. L. *College: The Undergraduate Experience in America.* New York: HarperCollins, 1987.

Cheney, L. *Fifty Hours: A Core Curriculum for Students.* Washington, D.C.: National Endowment for the Humanities, 1989.

Gaff, J. G. *New Life for the College Curriculum: Assessing Achievements and Furthering Progress in the Reform of General Education.* San Francisco: Jossey-Bass, 1991.

Gamson, Z. E. *Higher Education in the Real World: The Story of CAEL.* Wolfeboro, N.H.: Longwood Academic, 1989.

Graff, G. *Beyond the Culture Wars: How Teaching the Conflicts Can Revitalize American Education.* New York: Norton, 1992.

Haworth, J. G., and Conrad, C. F. *Emblems of Quality in Higher Education: Developing and Sustaining High-Quality Programs.* Needham Heights, Mass.: Allyn & Bacon, 1997.

Johnson, D. K. "General Education 2000—A National Survey: How General Education Changed Between 1989 and 2000." Unpublished doctoral dissertation, Pennsylvania State University, 2003.

Lindquist, J. "Strategies for Change." In J. G. Gaff, J. L. Ratcliff, and Associates (eds.), *Handbook of the Undergraduate Curriculum.* San Francisco: Jossey-Bass, 1997.

Newton, R. R. "Tensions and Models in General Education Planning." *Journal of General Education,* 2001, *49*(3), 165–181.

Ratcliff, J. L. "What Is a Curriculum and What Should It Be?" In J. G. Gaff, J. L. Ratcliff, and Associates (eds.), *Handbook of Undergraduate Curriculum: Innovation and Reform.* San Francisco: Jossey-Bass, 1997.

Ratcliff, J. L. "A Model for Understanding Curricular Coherence and Transparency." Paper presented at the Annual EAIR Forum, Freie Universitat Berlin, Germany, Sept. 7, 2000.

Ratcliff, J. L., Johnson, D. K., La Nasa, S. M., and Gaff, G. J. *The Status of General Education in the Year 2000: Summary of a National Survey.* Washington, D.C.: Association of American Colleges and Universities, 2001.

Senge, P. M. "The Leader's New Work. Building Learning Organizations." In T. Jick (ed.), *Managing Change.* Homewood, Ill.: Irwin, 1993.

Stark, J. S., and Lattuca, L. R. *Shaping the College Curriculum: Academic Plans in Action.* Needham Heights, Mass.: Allyn & Bacon, 1997.

Study Group on the Conditions of Excellence in American Higher Education. *Involvement in Learning: Realizing the Potential of American Higher Education.* Washington, D.C.: National Institute of Education, 1984.

Tyler, R. *Basic Principles of Curriculum Development.* Chicago: University of Chicago Press, 1950.

Weingartner, R. *Undergraduate Curriculum: Goals and Means.* Washington, D.C.: American Council on Education/Oryx Press, 1993.

Zemsky, R. *Structure and Coherence: Measuring the Undergraduate Curriculum.* Washington, D.C.: Association of American Colleges, 1989.

D. KENT JOHNSON *is director of assessment services at the Arkansas State University, Jonesboro, Arkansas.*

JAMES L. RATCLIFF *is president and senior consultant, Performance Associates Postsecondary Consulting, Pueblo West, Colorado.*

Change in general education is changing, and there are lessons to be learned in reenvisioning the curriculum.

Re-envisioning the Change Process in General Education

James L. Ratcliff

Planning has played an ever increasing role in the reform of general education. The majority of those undertaking change in the past decade, as reported by the CAO 2000 and GE 2000 surveys (Johnson, 2003; Ratcliff, Johnson, La Nasa, and Gaff, 2001), did so by linking general education closely to institutional mission. Changes in the general education curricula at Franklin Pierce, American, and Hamline were undertaken in part to relate the program to institutional mission better. Cascadia's general education goals were derived from institutional mission.

Many of the innovative and imaginative curricula of the past decade came about in the absence of systematic planning, program review, or assessments of student learning; yet as general education has increased in priority across campuses, increasingly it has become subject to more formal planning and review processes. Simultaneously, the grand redesign of curricula and programs has given way to a new incrementalism of change based on assessment and review, self-study, and overall institutional strategy, of which general education is regarded as but a piece. Over the past two decades and across the globe, planning and evaluation processes have been implemented, then modified, replaced, or augmented with more stringent policies and procedures (Neave and van Vught, 1994). Change in general education has followed these patterns.

How Changing the Curriculum Has Changed over the Decade

Between 1984 and 1994, over twenty national reports and proposals for reform were issued (Stark and Lattuca, 1997). These reports were generally critical of the undergraduate curriculum and had specific relevance to general education. The reports proposed knowledge, skills, or experiences that should be common to undergraduate education and advocated various specific elements of the curriculum—core requirements, collaborative learning, and assessment of outcomes, to name a few—as essential or desired ways of improving educational practice. Most important, they set the stage and channeled the discourse on general education reform that was occurring across campuses during the 1990s. In many respects, the shape, character, and direction of the reforms followed those advocated by these national reports.

In *To Reclaim a Legacy: A Report on the Humanities in Higher Education* (1984), the director of the National Endowment for the Humanities, William Bennett, argued that student election of course work resulted in a disintegration of the humanities core; he proposed a core curriculum of great books as the cure. *Involvement in Learning* (1984), a National Institute on Education report on the conditions of excellence in higher education, found undergraduate curricula to be fragmented and not engaging or enlightening to students; it urged "clearly expressed, publicly announced, and consistently maintained standards of performance for awarding degrees—standards that are based on societal and institutional definitions of college-level academic learning" (pp. 15–16). It would have change in general education begin with clearly defined and communicated curricular goals and standards.

Ernest Boyer (1987), president of the Carnegie Council for the Advancement of Teaching, pointed to curricular friction between career and liberal learning aims of college and promoted the integration of disciplinary knowledge into seven areas of inquiry that all students should experience. *Integrity in the College Curriculum* (Association of American Colleges, 1985) advocated that students be provided with experiences leading to the development of abilities rather than be given traditional introductions to the disciplines. *Integrity* claimed nine such experiences were essential for a broad and relevant collegiate education: inquiry, literacy, understanding numerical data, historical consciousness, science, values, art, international and multicultural experiences, and study in depth.

In 1989, Lynn Cheney, director of the National Endowment for the Humanities, campaigned for a prescribed curriculum, referred to by the title of her book, *50 Hours*, to improve students' knowledge of literature, philosophy, institutions, and art in their own and other cultures. Bloom's widely read *The Closing of the American Mind* (1987) argued for a return to a great books curriculum based on Western values.

The importance of teaching about other peoples and cultures was a focal point of debate. D'Souza (1991) insisted that the inclusion of diversity courses had split institutions of higher education on moral grounds, leaving them inherently racist, sexist, homophobic, and class based. In contrast, the 1995 report by the Association of American Colleges and Universities, *American Pluralism and the College Curriculum*, recommended that every institution include a course that is "an extended and comparative exploration of diverse peoples in this society; with significant attention to their differing experiences of United States democracy" (p. 25).

The impact of the reports was not uniformly manifest in curricular changes. Credits allotted to general education in the baccalaureate degree never rose to Lynn Cheney's desired fifty, and the core curricula that she, Bloom, and Bennett advocated were not widely adopted. Assessment of student learning outcomes as urged by *Involvement in Learning* has yet to be fully adopted. Nevertheless, the changes to general education over the decade did clarify goals, limit student course choices, refocus programs from the introduction to disciplines to interdisciplinary groupings around themes, clusters, and learning communities, and courses on diversity widely became part of most programs. Students' skills, capacities, abilities, proficiencies, and talents became far more important. Less fragmentation, more coherence, and active learning were the broad aims of the changes undertaken. It was a decade of broad, reflective reforms set afoot by a national debate and a heightened priority given to undergraduate education.

Perhaps of equal significance is how these changes came about. In the late 1980s, national reports stimulated debate and discussion across campuses and within the major associations of higher education. For example, an Association of American Colleges and Universities (AAC&U) annual meeting served as catalyst for the remaking of general education at Portland State University. The university's faculty were introduced to the national discourse on the undergraduate curriculum, came to recognize that there was a referent literature on effective undergraduate learning, and began to consider what a complete overhaul of the general education curriculum might look like (Reardon and Ramaley, 1997). These events and their parallels were replayed across the country as campuses engaged in discussions, reviewed research, garnered counsel from consultants, and crafted new curricula. The bases of change were the imagination of campus leaders and the affirmation of associated research on good practices. By and large, change was not necessarily a result of strategic plans, program reviews, or student assessments. Examples are manifest in this volume: the Hamline Plan, the Pierce Plan, the reform model at American University, and more recently, the "Cascadia way." Broadly, they are also the reforms and results benchmarked in the GE 2000 and CAO 2000 surveys.

While this may have been the profile and pathway to change in the late 1980s and throughout the 1990s, it is not necessarily how change is proceeding today. As the reforms of the 1990s were taking root, other changes also were adopted in college administration that had import for how change in general education was to proceed in the foreseeable future. The general education reforms of the 1990s fully embraced the nomenclature of goal setting, goal clarity, harmony of goals to mission, and the linkage of goals to requirements. Today, strategic planning, program evaluation, assessment, and continuous quality enhancement frame curricular reform and quicken the pace of change, making it an ongoing process. Guy Neave was first to note, warily, the emergence of the "evaluative state" in higher education (1998, p. 278). While the GE 2000 and CAO 2000 surveys uncovered few reforms initiated from program reviews or assessments of student learning, it is clear from their reports that today's general education programs are subject to such reviews and incorporate student assessments (however incompletely) as well.

While the pace and intensity of planning and evaluation activities have accelerated greatly, their record in improving general education programs and the students enrolled in them is less clear. The question is open as to whether the current processes of academic planning and evaluation, now so firmly entrenched, have specific limitations in the improvement of quality in general education and in the learning of students.

Program Improvement as a Quality Enhancement Activity

Unfortunately, program quality itself is a problematic concept. A variety of scholars have approached the topic, but the definitional dilemma is portrayed well in Robert Pirsig's *Zen and the Art of Motorcycle Maintenance*:

> Quality. . . . you know what it is, yet you don't know what it is. But that's self-contradictory. But when you try to say what the quality is, apart from things that have it, it all goes poof! There's nothing to talk about. But if you can't say what Quality is, how do you know what it is, then for all practical purposes, it doesn't exist at all. . . .
>
> But for all practical purposes it really does exist. What else are the grades based on? Why else would people pay fortunes for some things and throw others in the trash pile? Obviously, some things are better than others. . . . but what's the "betterness"? . . . So round and round you go, spinning mental wheels, and nowhere finding any place to get traction. What the hell is Quality? [1974, p. 179]

It is this contradictory nature of quality that has real and practical consequences for the reform of general education, and it has specific implications for the extended use of the planning and evaluation paradigm in general education change. Purpose relative to quality helps define the direction of programs. Rudolph noted, "In describing its structure, we compute courses, semesters, lectures, departments, majors, and so forth. In exploring the substance of the curriculum, the stuff of which the learning and teaching is made, we are in the presence of quality, whether good or bad. . . . Judging quality requires some notion of what the curriculum is expected to do" (1997, p. 2). As Rudolph notes, structure and substance are two different program attributes, quality and quality improvement pertaining largely to the latter.

Lee Harvey's review of literature (1997) points to multiple, not always harmonious, views of program quality:

- Quality—meaning the *exceptional*, where quality is related to the conception of excellence
- Quality—meaning *perfection*, where quality has consistent and error-free attributes
- Quality—meaning *fit for purpose*, where quality fulfills the perceived requirements of stakeholders
- Quality—meaning *value*, where a government agency, subsidizing employer, or agency finds optimum benefit relative to cost
- Quality—meaning *transformation*, where quality necessarily involves a change from a current to an ideal end state

The Pierce Plan (described in Chapter Two) was created to make the college distinctive from its competitors and thus attract students (quality as being exceptional). It also sought to use best practices in undergraduate education (quality as perfection). The Hamline Plan (explored in Chapter Five) also sought to be a distinctive program stressing "practical liberal arts" (being exceptional), but the reform also came about because the old curriculum was judged out of date and not tied to institutional mission (quality as fit for purpose). The reforms at American University (set out in Chapter Three) were to craft a distinctive curriculum (being exceptional) and to increase rigor (perfection) and coherence (quality as fit for purpose). Cascadia (described in Chapter Four) designed a curriculum derived of its mission (fit for purpose) while meeting requirements for transfer and articulation (quality as value). Both Hamline and American found that the full ramification and requirements of the reforms originally implemented became known only as each program evolved (quality as transformation). Thus, changing general education to improve program quality and the associated student experience takes multiple directions and calls for discourse on different visions of what quality is. This, in turn, determines how change is envisioned and implemented.

Program Improvement as an Academic Planning and Management Activity

Planning and evaluation models typically examine the structure and functions of general education. American University, for example, began its reforms by deriving goals from institutional values and course objectives from program goals. It divided the realms of knowledge into five areas and allocated a maximum of 150 courses to service those areas. Changing the structure and function of general education resulted clearly in a more viable program. The use of academic planning models in changing general education curriculum was increasingly prevalent during the 1990s.

Also useful was the formalization of governance relative to general education. Many institutions provided ongoing administrative leadership for general education, including a dean or director of general education and directors of writing, first-year seminars, and other components to complement the institution-wide committee for general education. With individuals specifically assigned to provide leadership, general education was more likely to remain an institutional priority and have continuous direction to maintain its vitality.

However, structural and functional changes to general education may not fully address those factors or forces hindering or facilitating student learning. Functional and structural changes rely on a predetermined formal order. Adopting a common format for core courses, for example, may bring greater curricular consistency but not necessarily greater student engagement. As academic planning becomes formalized, so do the solutions emanating from it. The result may generate positive incremental changes but may be of limited use when the charge is to rethink or remake general education as a whole.

The problem of transformation, by its very nature, calls for moving beyond the current established order. If the existing design, structure, or function fails to engage, enlighten, and enliven students and faculty adequately, then it may not be the best starting point for reenvisioning the curriculum. Similarly, using the same academic planning model to generate a new general education reform may mask the source of problems in the old and embed those problems in the new. The literature on program redesign is replete with examples of failed change of this nature (Corder, Horsburgh, and Melrose, 1999; Toombs, 1977–1978; Toombs and Tierney, 1991; Trowler and Knight, 1999).

George Mason University used the academic planning model of Ralph Tyler in designing its often-cited general education curriculum (Blois, 1987). Tyler (1950) proposed that quality curricula possessed clearly stated and interrelated purposes, processes, organization, and evaluation. More recently, the ideas of Stark and Lattuca (1997) have been widely used in academic planning. They also advocate systematic curricular planning of structure and function, including description of purpose, content, sequence, learners, instructional resources, evaluation, and adjustment. The model has proven useful for design and evaluation of curriculum at the levels of lessons, courses, programs, and institutional academic plans. Stark and Lattuca also recognized certain "dynamic issues" in academic planning, "especially those that involve the interactions of people and the processes that concern people" (p. 378).

In general education, academic plans have provided a reliable and consistent way of designing and evaluating curricula. They call attention to the purpose and organization of the program, number and types of courses included, and how it is to be evaluated and adjusted to achieve its goals and objectives (Stark and Lattuca, 1997). The GE 2000 and CAO 2000 surveys indicated that campus leaders worked to link general education goals to institutional mission, clarified those goals, and specified curricular requirements that met those goals. These actions, based largely on an academic planning framework, helped free general education from disciplinary turf wars and introductory courses arranged in distributional smorgasbords and permitted the creation of interdisciplinary courses clustered together in sequence through themes and learning communities. Academic planning models that stress structure and function may have been the right approach for the time. Yet more of the same medicine may not be the best prescription for the lingering maladies of general education. Recall that a principal aim of the reforms of the past decade was to make general education more coherent, yet only 38 percent of chief academic officers (CAOs) in the CAO 2000 survey said their plans achieved this.

Program Improvement as a Relational Activity

Persistent problems of linking coherence and student engagement may benefit from a fresh approach to general education reform. An alternative is to envision general education reform as a relational communication process. Howard (1991), for example, contends that general education could be better understood through Jürgen Habermas's theory of communicative competence. Applebee (1996) sees curriculum as a conversation between teachers and learners, representing "traditions of knowing and doing" (p. 35). The process of improving general education involves transactions among stakeholders where fields of knowledge, sets of skills, values associated with intellectual inquiry, and personal development get defined through discourse (Ratcliff, 2000, 2001, 2003). Curricular design is an act of communication involving oral (through advising, for example) and written (through the catalogue, for example) representations of institutional policies and practices in settings of dynamic discourse (the general education task force meetings). Changes in general education are dialogic in that they are shaped by the change process itself, the actors or stakeholders in that process, and their socially constructed understanding of what a quality program is.

What is a quality general education program? The word *quality* refers to an attribute or set of attributes. Individually and collectively, people select and assemble the attributes that constitute quality. The quality attributes a politician may associate with general education (such as the number of hours required and its effect on time to degree) may be different from those of students (which may encompass connection to career, interactions with the instructor, and assignments required). As the quality attributes are selected, the individual constructs meaning around the idea of general education, which serves as a filter to subsequent information regarding the program. Each stakeholder constructs an idea of program quality from a few select attributes, with those attributes varying from stakeholder to stakeholder.

Program quality and change therefore are not only individual and personal but also social and dynamic. Faculty members' discussions with peers and students and students' interactions with fellow students and faculty influence the construction of what general education means on a day-to-day basis. How individuals across campus assemble their understanding of general education constitutes the communicative and relational dimension of the curriculum (Ratcliff, 2001).

General education is an organization of knowledge. Its basic building blocks are courses. Courses have conventionally been aligned with how disciplines organize knowledge (Clark, 1983), but as the GE 2000 survey shows, they are increasingly clustered across disciplines according to themes to be socially or personally relevant. The quality of general education courses, individually and collectively, is influenced strongly by the formal and informal communication of departments. Advisers may tell students to avoid a course, get it out of the way, or select it as an important complement to their program. Faculty peers develop high regard for courses and sequences that convey their rigor and relevance. This communication facilitates multiple social interactions fundamental to teaching, learning, and research. Such communication is the basis for the socialization and intellectual development of students (Trowler and Knight, 1999).

The complexities of communication are important to making changes in general education. The students, the faculty, and the administration, writ large, will attach interpretation to the reports of the general education committee, the discourse about general education in faculty meetings, students' electronic assessment portfolios, and the like. The extent to which communication engenders understanding and conveys the values of the program is critical. Students first encounter general education in their undergraduate program, and the first years of college are where most dropouts occur. For most institutions, student success, retention, and thus tuition revenue are fundamental to their political and economic well-being.

Quality as a Social Construct

What is and is not seen as a quality general education program is very much the result of educational philosophy, beliefs, values, normative positions, and power within and between departments within the institutions and among institutions competing for students and resources (Barnett, 1992; Fuhrmann and Grasha, 1983; van Vught, 1994). The Pierce and Hamline plans, for example, were to be distinctive programs, helping prospective students and their parents distinguish their undergraduate programs from others. These curricula were intended to be personal and social constructs meaningful to their stakeholders.

A curriculum represents knowledge, culture, scholarship, and perspective from which students of various backgrounds, interests, and abilities experience, discover, and gain understanding (Shulman, 1987; Ratcliff, 1997). When individual faculty members create the curriculum as an atomistic assemblage of single courses, lectures, and seminars, the quality of the curriculum as a whole is problematic. Quality becomes embedded in the various values and expectations of individual faculty rather than the faculty as a whole. The result is a general education similar to that at Hamline prior to reform, a "two of everything" program that students "got out of the way" rather than regarded as a meaningful learning experience. Such a distributional program provides students with little guidance in improving their learning and little common ground as to its outcomes. The quality of general education is as much a social construct as is the institution in which it is organized (Clark, 1983; van Vught, 1994).

Relational Dialectics and the Study of Contradictions

These observations regarding change in general education are drawn from relational dialectics (Altman, Vinsel, and Brown, 1981; Baxter and Montgomery, 1996). From this perspective, general education and the undergraduate experience exist through people's communication with one another, wherein they articulate multiple and opposing tendencies. Discussions of general education are social discourses that are unfinished and ongoing and involve "a polyphony of dialectical voices" (Baxter and Montgomery, 1996, p. 4) all struggling to be heard, and through that struggle, the stage for future struggles is established. The Association of American Colleges' *A New Vitality in General Education* made a similar point: "Tensions exist over what to teach and how to teach; whether great books or contemporary literature should be selected as texts; how much and what type of in-class and out-of-class learning should be included; how to best address individual and community needs in the curriculum; and what students want and what institutions think students need" (1988, p. 5). While certain issues are easily accessible through structural solutions, others are not. If certain students are underprepared in the mathematics, remediation may logically follow. If assessments show that students need to improve their writing, strengthening the writing program may be an appropriate step. Yet broad campus and social concerns about curricular quality and coherence emerge from tensions endemic to the concepts themselves and are not so simply solved. Oppositions regarding such issues as quality or coherence generate a dynamic that both propels and impedes change. The disciplinary department and major are specific centrifugal weights on general education (Gaff, 1991).

Contradictions, Oppositions, and Change in General Education

Contradictions and tensions, such as the prescription or election of courses, disciplinary and interdisciplinary learning, learning organized by cohorts of students and that arranged by sequence of subjects, are inherent in general education. Contradictions from this vantage point are not necessarily failures or inadequacies or targets for resolution or consensus. They also are the basic drivers of both incremental and transformative change (Baxter and Montgomery, 1996; Ratcliff, 2003).

Individuals find themselves in contradictory or conflicting roles when discussing, designing, and implementing change in general education. Faculty members recruited to represent their various fields of study are asked to reduce, condense, and translate their fields into modules that fit into interdisciplinary sequences, first-year seminars, and learning communities. In a single Franklin Pierce course, for example, faculty teach art, music, history, literature, and philosophy, drawing from the language of the specialists and disciplinarians, translating and synthesizing to the second-year undergraduates. Students create electronic portfolios in which this knowledge is interpreted and fused. Victoria Richart led the design of Cascadia's unique educational program, but she also must relate its features to accrediting standards and transfer requirements of the statewide coordinating board. Such tensions and opposing issues breed role conflict within and among the stakeholders in the change process (Katz and Kahn, 1978; King and King, 1990).

Contradictory roles represent the dynamic interplay of competing forces manifest in the thoughts and discourse of an individual. Roles are contradictory when they involve opposites that "are actively incompatible and mutually negate one another" (Baxter and Montgomery, 1996, p. 8). While opposites are important to curricular change, not all opposites are the same. A *logical opposite* involves a concept or issue and its absence; coherence and fragmentation (X and not X) are *logical opposites*. A *functional opposite* involves two distinct concepts or issues that function in incompatible ways, negating each other. Access and assessment provide an example of functional opposition. Assessing student learning on entry to college may help detect those students who are underprepared, but it may also discourage student enrollment among those at risk and who fear testing, thereby suppressing the number of underprepared students taking the assessment. Functional opposites lack negation as the basis of their opposition. Assessment does not negate access, or vice versa. Such functional oppositions also exist in a nondichotomous or nonbipolar environment. Few colleges can choose not to assess their students (due to accreditation standards), but they can choose how and what to assess. Few can effectively avoid serving underprepared students, but institutional policies and programs can be crafted to serve well those who enter without sufficient precollegiate education to succeed. If-then thinking and dualistic thinking will not lead to viable solutions to such problems (Altman, Vinsel, and Brown, 1981; Baxter and Montgomery, 1996). Confusing functional oppositions for logical opposites can impede the change process. Distributional plans and prescribed core curriculums are frequently portrayed as logical opposites in the general education. During the 1990s, many institutions decided that their distributional plans allowed a high degree of student choice, contributed to curricular fragmentation, and resulted in a lack of clarity of purpose. This was the case at both American and Hamline universities prior to the changes that these institutions undertook. Yet most of the curricular revisions of the decade chose a third way—courses clustered by theme—rather than shift to either logical opposite: a prescribed core as the preferred solution. Prescription and election were but one dimension of a functional opposition; another dimension was coherence, as was discussed in Chapter Six.

Conventional approaches to logical and conceptual oppositions involve efforts to eliminate them, usually through consensual decision making. However, each concept derives its meaning from one or more opposing concepts, issues, or characteristics. For example, the concept of a capstone course comes in part from the lack of synthesis among disparate courses. Organizing central concepts such as great books or key competencies presume curricula where student election is a predominant feature or central purposes are not articulated. This oppositional dynamic is part of the identity of each general education component and shapes the roles of individuals in teaching, learning, or changing general education.

The unity of conceptual oppositions illustrates how social dynamics may have both-and rather than either-or attributes. With regard specifically to change in general education, Gaff previously noted, "The issues are often posed as mutually exclusive alternatives: knowledge *versus* skills, Western *versus* non-Westerner cultures, the traditional canon *versus* new scholarship that challenges traditional assumptions. One need not be a genius to know that it is possible to have both. . . . Indeed, a successful strategy to reform the curriculum demands a 'both-and' rather than an 'either-or' approach" (1991, p. 29).

Institutions and programs must contend with this Janus both-and attribute of general education and the quality of learning and the nature of the learning environment that result (Baxter and Montgomery, 1996; Elton, 2002; Ratcliff, 2001). This observation does not portend merely to the resolution of areas of contention in the curriculum but also to the way we understand change itself.

Understanding Change as a Dialectic Process

The wholesale remaking of general education, as we have seen in the case stories from Hamline and Franklin Pierce, exemplify transformative change. Academic folklore tells of a wise professor who remarked, "When change occurs, things are different." Much of what we expect from rethinking general education is realized from the bottom up. Yet certain aspects require further modification and fine-tuning, others perform not as planned, and the results generate discourse leading to new changes previously not envisioned. Several campuses implementing learning communities or student portfolios as assessment mechanisms report the faculty time required to carry out each of these innovations far exceeds what had been anticipated. Many yearn for change but expect their daily lives to go about uninterrupted.

Both change and stability are inherent in social systems. General education reforms are intended as improvements. Yet change and stability as a dialectic unity of oppositions occur through the interplay of campus conventions and curricular transformation. When Harvard and Stanford made changes to general education in the 1980s, they were widely watched because the reforms were anticipated to be pacesetters to their traditions of quality; the notions of change and stability are inexorably intertwined in discussions of program improvement.

The role of the disciplines is invariably a focal point in discussions about changing general education. One CAO 2000 respondent commented that his institution "will continue to hire and develop disciplinary experts rather than generalists," and coherence in general education will be achieved "not by blending substance and crossing disciplinary lines but by establishing a common form for all core courses." Here stability is embodied in the very characteristics of a discipline (Ratcliff, 2000). The terms, concepts, models, themes, and theories used, the modes and methods of inquiry employed, and the conventions regarding arriving at conclusions and constructing generalizations are components of disciplines that add stability to discourse. Also, curricula do more than embody professors' interpretations of recurring teaching and learning situations. Curricula also guide interactions in teaching and learning situations so that they resemble each other in premeditated ways. As the classroom changes materially (as in the addition of technology) and in the students' and professors' perceptions of it, the categories of knowledge and the representation of them undergo ongoing, incremental change (Ratcliff, 2001). Thus, discourse about the role of disciplines in general education necessarily accommodates both stability and change.

Conventional views of change see it as the overcoming of the status quo. By adopting interdisciplinary course clusters, the influence of departments and disciplines will be removed—or will it? Without faculty development to accompany a new interdisciplinary, clustered curriculum, instructors may gravitate toward familiar territory, asking students to do the synthesis of fields of knowledge while they teach from the paradigms and content of their fields. To bring about true interdisciplinary teaching, curricular change should be regarded more holistically, attending to more than the structure of the program. So what might be an alternative, more holistic view of change?

Aristotle made a distinction between efficient causation and formal causation that is useful here. Efficient causation describes cumulative cause-effect relationships. Formal causation refers to patterns of relationships among phenomena (Rychlak, 1977). Efficient causation is at the heart of strategic plans, program reviews, and assessments of student learning. General education reform, in contrast, often involves questions of formal causation: how things and people fit together into patterns, how programs and people develop over time, and how patterns within the institution or among students and academics shift and change. In formal causation, no single component or person is changed by any single prior event or factor. Oppositions are not independent change agents in formal causal situations in the conventional sense of independent variables whose effects on other phenomena can be measured (Baxter and Montgomery, 1996). They are endemic to discourse and change and fit into holistic patterns. A leadership challenge is to capture and portray oppositional dynamics as they evolve among students and staff, among departments and divisions, between general education and other curricular and extracurricular components. To understand change from a relational viewpoint is to focus on how people and events interact rather than on how one policy, person, or event changed the program.

A central question in many general education reforms is whether the focus should be on the improvement process itself or a set of desired outcomes. The latter presumes a teleological aim; that is, change is to be directed toward an ideal end state. Great books curricula strive for ideals framed as what students should know; competency-based curricula endeavor to teach students a specific set of skills and abilities. Both aim for an ideal state. The general education program, its instructional staff, and the students enrolled are judged relative to the attainment of the course and program goals on the assumption that they will be pulled toward the attainment of these goals as ideal outcomes.

In contrast, learning communities are implemented to ensure that students encounter the curriculum together as a cohort. Internships provide students with an experience related to the world of work, the outcome of which may or may not have precise objectives tied tightly to content or skill goals, and student portfolios may ask students to make judgments about their best work rather than provide a basis for determining how well the general education program is achieving its goals. Cascadia's Teaching and Learning Academy and Employee Learning Institute and American University's General Education Faculty Assistance Program and Center for Teaching Excellence are units designed to facilitate change and improvement. These innovations put improvement processes in place and are judged by the extent to which these processes lead to improvement. From this vantage point, change is not driven by a particular ideal (other than "improvement is good"). Change is manifest in ongoing processes that simply bring the program, its faculty, and its students to different intermediate places along a longer road of enhanced general education.

Transcendent change is where the general direction is known, but because the changes are so profound, the shape and nature of the outcomes are not known (Toombs and Tierney, 1991). In many respects, this is how the 1984–1985 Hamline reforms were characterized. With transcendent change, the thesis-antithesis-synthesis dynamic is breached, and new paradigms for understanding emerge (Baxter and Montgomery, 1996; Kuhn, 1962). While the Hamline reforms included interdisciplinary course work, only recently has campus discourse refocused on the pedagogy of interdisciplinary teaching and learning.

Not everyone subscribes to transcendent change, supporting in its place a continuous process model of change. Certainly, the majority of change reported in the GE 2000 survey was not the grand redesign of general education leading to a signature curriculum and the remaking of the institutional culture. General education reforms, transcendent or incremental, may or may not result in progress.

Often reform efforts generate a sense of curricular churning rather than programmatic progress. A worthwhile distinction can be made between cyclical and cumulative change. Cyclical change is that distinguished by a recurring pattern. The dynamics of reform discourse moves from one opposition to another and then back again. Such movement reifies concepts and understanding, may generate a sense of churning about an issue, but may result in a redefinition of the relationship of opposing concepts or issues (Altman, Vinsel, and Brown, 1981; Baxter and Montgomery, 1996; Werner and Baxter, 1994). Conventional views of general education reform have described it as a "perennial" (Newton 2001) or an episodic activity resulting from the interplay of faculty committees and administrative resolve, leading to program revision or redesign.

Cumulative change is a progression of nonrecurring actions through which the program, its faculty, and its students are permanently altered. The change can be viewed as a positive, negative, or neutral occurrence, but its result becomes lasting. The reforms at Franklin Pierce College and American and Hamline universities permanently changed general education; what followed were evolutionary refinements of those reforms. Cumulative change, like its cyclical opposite, can be found in both transcendent or process models of change.

General education reform inherently entails change processes that, more often than not, comprise formal causation rather than simple, efficient cause-and-effect relationships. Yet campus discussions gravitate toward the simple cause-and-effect characterization of change, oversimplifying the relationships. State legislatures or higher education governing boards may mandate that certain subjects be taught in general education or that it consist of a set number of credit hours, such as has occurred recently in New York, Illinois, and Colorado, assuming these will cause improved student learning. Cause-and-effect explanations like these grossly simplify such situations. The complexities of program improvement activities require consideration of multiple, conflicting forces and views to effect meaningful reform. When change becomes cyclical, it does not mean that it is unproductive thrashing about or that it will not lead to improvement. When change is cumulative, it does not guarantee improvement either. The nature of change can be neither presumed nor ignored in curriculum reform activities.

People, Praxis, and Change

People are proactive agents in the change process. Yet remarkably, people—students, faculty, and academic leaders—are often viewed as passive dependent or independent variables (Pascarella and Terenzini, 1991; Stark and Lattuca, 1997; Toombs, 1977–1978). The dynamic, interactive communication of individuals is a precursor to the choices and actions taken by those people, who in turn shape the change process. *Praxis* is a term used to describe the effects and actions of people engaged in discourse (Baxter and Montgomery, 1996). The students joining in a learning community form peer structures for study groups, recreation, and socializing. Social life is essentially recursive of academic life; what people do in teaching, learning, and socializing and what social structures are intended by general education (such as learning communities, interdisciplinarity, and teamwork) are implicated by each other. People are both proactive and reactive as ideas and actions are shared among the stakeholders, and their identities become reified in normative and institutional practices such as the general education program.

Reification involves the development of patterns of thought and behavior that extend to and guide future ideas and actions. Reification leads to conventions and traditions that provide a certain amount of stability in stability-change dynamics. Institutional policies and practices, such as general education, consist of the rules, rituals, and routines of academic life (Cohen and March, 1986). As structural frameworks within which change may occur, they may appear to stakeholders as reified norms that understate their "changeable, flexible and plastic" nature (Bakhtin, 1986, p. 80). The divisions of knowledge in the curriculum, or the number of credits assigned to a particular division, may appear sacrosanct, inhibiting the committee charged with revision to overlook a full range of choices in the change process. This may explain why general education is thought to be such a knotty issue, such a difficult part of the curriculum to change, and yet the GE 2000 survey reports four out of five colleges and universities undertaking change in general education.

Reification of thought and action has been observed within the academic disciplines (Ratcliff, 2001) and has been demonstrated in research on proposal writing, student essays, and the evolution of drafts of scholarly articles submitted and then revised for publication (Berkenkotter and Huckin, 1995). Change proceeds through a process of reification wherein disciplinary and administrative rules, rituals, and routines constrain the interactive and dynamic communication of choices by stakeholders in the change process. However, these same people give life to the oppositions that challenge conventions, affirm the plasticity of the social organism, and make it possible to bring about change. The very forces most often cited as forms and sources of intractability also provide the impetus for change. Each of the actors challenges the reification of actions governed by institutional norms, disciplinary boundaries, and departmental prerogatives. For example, one respondent in the CAO 2000 survey reported that the "current curriculum is out-of-date and does not address coherency or needs, also does not have adequate assessment." The inadequacies of the past (dated, lacks coherence) and the needs of the future (student centered, assessments) propel the changes of the present. Every exchange among stakeholders is informed by past exchanges and shapes future ones as well (Baxter and Montgomery, 1996). Documenting the inadequacies of the current curriculum and the future needs that the reform should address are useful activities in bringing about meaningful changes.

Holistic Understanding

Viewing general education as a set of interactive and iterative relationships requires us to see the reform process holistically. As my colleague Jerry Gaff has recently said, "It is a constant challenge for the faculty as a whole to take responsibility for the curriculum as a whole. Engaging faculty understanding of, and support for, general education is an unending task" (Gaff, 1991, p. 31). People, programs, and perspectives need to be understood in their relationship to one another. A holistic view, then, is not merely a comprehensive one but also one that views a social environment as a series of relationships, processes, interactions, and interdependencies. This raises three important issues: how conceptual oppositions and issues are situated relative to the change, the nature of their interdependence, and the context within which they interact (Baxter and Montgomery, 1996).

To understand how oppositions are situated, our focus needs to be on the interplay and interaction of individuals and not on the individuals in isolation, whether students, academic staff, or administrators. Change involves more than merely stating a clear educational goal to which faculty teach and students learn; it also attends to how that goal is discussed and understood by faculty and by students and how it becomes manifest in the course work required. To elaborate, student learning alone should not be the focus of general education reform either generically ("What is an educated person?") or particularly ("Students should be able to think critically and analytically"). Rather, to understand the change process, we also need to understand such learning in the context of student interactions with other students, faculty, staff, and administrators. Through these interactions, past exchanges shape communication, choices, and actions and influence future discourse, decisions, and directions. It is the interactions (and not merely the goal) that give shape to the extent that students and faculty become committed to lifelong learning or critical thinking from the general education program. Contemporary interactions develop patterns that extend to future actions. Close reading of a text, reflective discussions among peers and among students and mentors, and the habits of the mind and heart become socialized through the programs we create.

The interdependence of conceptual oppositions and issues is acted out situationally and contextually rather than generically: "As people come together in any social union, they create a host of dialectic forces" (Baxter and Montgomery, 1996, p. 15). The tensions in student, academic, staff, or administrative discourse get defined through the interplay and interaction of the actors involved. In general education courses, faculty members may be both experts (of specialties and as teachers) and learners (of interdisciplinarity, teamwork, curricular innovations in general education). Students can show what they know (demonstrating the mastery of the general education goal) and what they do not know (illustrating their own human deficiencies against the goals of the program). Such oppositions are both social and interpersonal, and the praxis of instruction reframes and redefines what is learned by whom and how.

Role conflict often results from this dialectic interplay of such oppositions. Those leading change need to guard against conceptual oppositions and issues emerging from the discourse about being reduced to stereotypes ("that's the position of administration") or interpersonal conflicts ("Ronald and Jeffrey always disagree about what should be expected of students"). As changes in general education proceed, oppositions among or between students, the faculty, and academic administrators need to be defined contextually ("What do Ronald's and Jeffrey's views tell us about setting academic standards?"). Therefore, those leading the reform effort must strive to keep the discourse holistic in perspective, focusing conversation on how the dynamics of interaction create impetus for change.

Another key reason that a holistic perspective is fundamental to the examination of past policies and practices and to the consideration of future program features is that social environments, including those fostered on campus, contain not one but multiple oppositions, most of which are of the both-and rather than the either-or variety. These oppositions are at the heart of change processes and may explain why the quotation from Prisig's *Zen and the Art of Motorcycle Maintenance* is so frequently used in discussions of quality and improvement.

Oppositions may be internal or external (Baxter and Montgomery, 1996). Internal oppositions, such as the extent to which student election should be part of the general education program, occur within the campus community. The general education program also may be subject to assessment criteria, credit hour limitations, or articulation agreements set by higher education coordinating or governing bodies. Employers may convey expectations of what all college graduates should know or be able to do, and the quality of high school writing, mathematics, or science curriculum may influence the knowledge, skills, and abilities of entering first-year students; these were external oppositions manifest in the development of curricula at Cascadia Community College. To account fully for oppositions—their interplay and their characteristics—a holistic view of the social environment is required of the academic leaders and committee or task force responsible for the review and reform of general education.

Finally, dialectic tensions in programmatic change vary from one context to another. In the CAO 2000 survey, one chief academic officer reported that curricular coherence was to be realized through a common format for all core courses in general education. A second CAO reported that the general education program seeks coherence through a "high level of integration among disciplines. . . . Our 'Making of the Modern Mind' [course] draws from 250 years of literature, philosophy, music, and history and is team taught by faculty from those areas." Looking at the catalogues of each institution would lead to the conclusion that general education programs share a similar core structure. Also, both rely on disciplinary specialists to realize their aims. Yet one strives for coherence through common course formatting, while the other attempts for the same curricular aim through interdisciplinary, team-taught courses. Thus, both the particulars and the generic qualities of the program relationships need careful study. The act of examining the educational program redefines its qualities, and undertaking program reviews necessarily fosters change. Such change may be simultaneously viewed as positive, negative, incidental, transformational, cyclical, or cumulative by the multitude of actors in the process; the tension among perspectives and the praxis of playing them out inevitably make differences occur, which then fuel the impetus to further change.

Conclusions

General education changed greatly over the decade 1900–2000, and equally significant is how changing the general education curriculum is evolving too. The transformative changes described in the Franklin Pierce, Hamline, and American case stories were deliberative and deliberate actions, but they were less tightly tied to formal program reviews, assessments of student learning, and budgeting and planning processes as were the refinements and enhancements to their plans that came later. As colleges and universities have adopted more formal models of planning and evaluation, general education reform has become caught up in these activities. A positive outcome has been less fragmented curricular and greater administrative oversight of the program as a whole and its many components (for example, with directors of the writing program and coordinators of first-year seminars). While a major motive for general education reform has been to create a more coherent curriculum, the changes reported in the GE 2000 and CAO 2000 surveys fell short of their mark in achieving greater coherence.

Curricular attributes such as coherence or distinctiveness may not be fully or adequately understood through analysis of the structure and organization of the curriculum, as academic planning and evaluation models lead us to do. Their shortcoming may be a result of the formal order they impose on the reform process, which predefines the framework for the change process, unwittingly replicating prior programmatic assumptions about how knowledge is organized and conveyed. Certainly, transformative changes are always "over the horizon" in that their implications cannot be fully envisioned at the outset of the change process. It is difficult to set goals and objectives, much less to measure their achievement relative to issues, dimensions, and attributes that are not yet fully known or understood. Staying the course—committing to change resulting from academic planning and program evaluation—no doubt will assist many in making ongoing and incremental improvements to general education. Such improvements, by definition, will be within the structure and function of current general education programs and may not effectively increase coherence or promulgate a distinctive or signature curriculum reflective of institutional values (Elton, 2002; Toombs, 1977–1978; Ratcliff, 2000, 2001, 2003).

Essentialist and prescriptive definitional approaches to general education provide abstract and theoretical exploration of issues but fail to capture the ways in which program improvement occurs situationally and contextually; the ways it is guided by the rules, rituals, and routines of the campus environment; how it extends past behaviors and events into patterns constraining contemporary thought and action regarding change; and the way it presupposes and defines new issues and future interactions as an impetus to change. Thus, viewing general education and change as relational dialectic processes may help see change as vibrant rather than merely episodic or ongoing. In the words of one of the CAO 2000 respondents, "The curriculum is dynamic; it requires constant revision and updating." Perhaps of greater significance, a relational perspective on general education reform also may assist in better understanding important curricular attributes, such as coherence, quality, and distinctiveness. Those who toil in the fields of program improvement and general education reform want their efforts to make a difference. Understanding how people and programs change through the dynamics of general education reform is a worthy and necessary aspiration, albeit one to which a proclamation of victory cannot yet be made, and perhaps never should be.

Our aims and expectations for general education are rightfully lofty. Its place in the culture of our institutions is so embedded that the assumptions on which it rests rarely go fully examined. General education today is like the furniture in our house, the groceries in the neighborhood store, and the paths across campus. We are so accustomed to where to sit and read a good book, in what aisle to find the cereal, and what pathways are pleasant for reflection or that make a quick shortcut to the lecture hall. The fundamental features of general education—its purposes, its practices, its rewards, its aims and the culture it seeks to foster—promise an extraordinary impact on how our students and our colleagues think, regard knowledge, lead and rely on one another, see the world and regard their role in it. With so much at stake, should not we take up the ongoing challenge of change in general education?

References

Altman, I., Vinsel, A., and Brown, B. B. "Dialectic Conceptions in Social Psychology: An Application to Social Penetration and Privacy Regulation." In L. Berkowitz (ed.), *Advances in Experimental Psychology*. Orlando, Fla.: Academic Press, 1981.

Applebee, A. N. *Curriculum as Conversation*. Chicago: University of Chicago Press, 1996.

Association of American Colleges. *Integrity in the College Curriculum: A Report to the Academic Community*. Washington, D.C.: American Association of Colleges, 1985.

Association of American Colleges. *A New Vitality in General Education*. Washington, D.C.: Association of American Colleges, 1988.

Association of American Colleges and Universities. *American Pluralism and the College Curriculum*. Washington, D.C.: Association of American Colleges and Universities, 1995.

Bakhtin, M. M. *Speech Genres and Other Late Essays* (V. W. McGee, trans.; C. Emerson and M. Holquist, eds.). Austin: University of Texas Press, 1986.

Barnett, R. *Improving Higher Education: Total Quality Care*. London: Society for Research in Higher Education and the Open University Press, 1992.

Baxter, L. A., and Montgomery, B. M. *Relating: Dialogues and Dialectics*. New York: Guilford Press, 1996.

Bennett, W. J. *To Reclaim a Legacy: A Report on the Humanities in Higher Education*. Washington, D.C.: National Endowment for the Humanities, 1984.

Berkenkotter, C., and Huckin, T. N. *Genre Knowledge in Disciplinary Communication: Cognition, Culture and Power*. Mahwah, N.J.: Erlbaum, 1995.

Blois, B. A., Jr. "The Page Program from Concept to Curriculum: George Mason University's Plan for Alternative General Education, 1981–1983." Unpublished doctor of education thesis, George Mason University, 1987.

Bloom, A. *The Closing of the American Mind: How Higher Education Has Failed Democracy and Impoverished the Souls of Today's Students*. New York: Simon & Schuster, 1987.

Boyer, E. L. *College: The Undergraduate Experience in America*. New York: HarperCollins 1987.

Cheney, L. *Fifty Hours: A Core Curriculum for Students*. Washington, D.C.: National Endowment for the Humanities, 1989.

Clark, B. R. *The Higher Education System: Academic Organization in a Cross-National Perspective*. Berkeley: University of California Press, 1983.

Cohen, M. D., and March, J. G. *Leadership and Ambiguity: The American College President*. (2nd ed.) Boston: Harvard Business School Press, 1986.

Corder, M., Horsburgh, M., and Melrose, M. "Quality Monitoring, Innovation and Transformative Learning." *Journal of Further and Higher Education*, 1999, 23(1), 101–108.

D'Souza, D. *Illiberal Education: The Politics of Race and Sex on Campus*. New York: Free Press, 1991.

Elton, L. "Quality Assurance Through Quality Enhancement." Paper presented at the annual EAIR Forum, European Association for Institutional Research, Prague, Sept. 9, 2002.

Furhmann, B. S., and Grasha, A. F. *College Teaching: A Practical Handbook*. New York: Little, Brown, 1983.

Gaff, J. G. *New Life for the College Curriculum: Assessing Achievements and Furthering Progress in the Reform of General Education.* San Francisco: Jossey-Bass, 1991.

Harvey, L. "External Quality Monitoring in the Market Place." *Tertiary Education and Management,* 1997, *3*(2), 25–35.

Howard, C. C. *Theories of General Education: A Critical Approach.* New York: Macmillan, 1991.

Katz, D., and Kahn, R. L. *The Social Psychology of Organizations.* (2nd ed.) New York: Wiley, 1978.

Johnson, D. K. "General Education 2000—A National Survey: How General Education Changed Between 1989 and 2000." Unpublished doctoral dissertation, Pennsylvania State University, 2003.

King, L. A., and King, D. W. "Role Conflict and Role Ambiguity: A Critical Assessment of Construct Validity." *Psychology Bulletin,* 1990, *107,* 48–64.

Kuhn, T. S. *The Structure of Scientific Revolutions.* Chicago: University of Chicago Press, 1962.

National Institute of Education. *Involvement in Learning: Realizing the Potential of American Higher Education: Report of the Study Group on Conditions of Excellence in American Higher Education.* Washington, D.C.: U.S. Government Printing Office, 1984.

Neave, G. "The Evaluative State Reconsidered." *European Journal of Education,* 1998, *33*(3), 265–84.

Neave, G., and van Vught, F. (eds.). *Prometheus Bound: The Changing Relationship Between Government and Higher Education in Western Europe.* New York: Pergamon Press, 1994.

Newton, R. R. "Tensions and Models in General Education Planning." *Journal of General Education,* 2001, *49*(3), 165–181.

Pascarella, E. T., and Terenzini, P. T. *How College Affects Students: Findings and Insights from Twenty Years of Research.* San Francisco: Jossey-Bass, 1991.

Pirsig, R. M. *Zen and the Art of Motorcycle Maintenance: An Inquiry into Values.* New York: Morrow, 1974.

Ratcliff, J. L. "What Is a Curriculum and What Should It Be?" In J. G. Gaff, J. L. Ratcliff, and Associates (eds.), *Handbook of Undergraduate Curriculum: Innovation and Reform.* San Francisco: Jossey-Bass, 1997.

Ratcliff, J. L. "A Model for Understanding Curricular Coherence and Transparency." Paper presented at the annual EAIR Forum, European Association for Institutional Research, Freie Universitat Berlin, Sept. 7, 2000.

Ratcliff, J. L. "Genre Knowledge and Curricular Excellence: An Examination of Curricular Dynamics and Curricular Grounding." Paper presented at the annual meeting of the Society for Research into Higher Education, Cambridge, England, Dec. 12, 2001.

Ratcliff, J. L. "Dynamic and Communicative Aspects of Quality Assurance." *Quality in Higher Education,* 2003, *9*(2), 117–131.

Ratcliff, J. L., Johnson, D. K., La Nasa, S. M., and Gaff, G. J. *The Status of General Education in the Year 2000: Summary of a National Survey.* Washington, D.C.: Association of American Colleges and Universities, 2001.

Reardon, M., and Ramaley, J. "Building Academic Community." In J. G. Gaff, J. L. Ratcliff, and Associates (eds.), *Handbook of the Undergraduate Curriculum.* San Francisco: Jossey-Bass, 1997.

Rudolph, F. *Curriculum: A History of the American Undergraduate Course of Study Since 1636.* San Francisco: Jossey-Bass, 1977.

Rychlak, J. F. *The Psychology of Vigorous Humanism.* (2nd ed.) New York: Wiley, 1977.

Shulman, L. S. "Knowledge and Teaching: Foundations of the New Reform." *Harvard Educational Review,* 1987, *57*(1), 1–22.

Stark, J. S., and Lattuca, L. R. *Shaping the College Curriculum: Academic Plans in Action.* Needham, Mass.: Allyn & Bacon, 1997.

Toombs, W. "The Application of Design-Based Curriculum to General Education." *Review of Higher Education,* 1977–1978, *1*(3), 18–29.

Toombs, W., Fairweather, J. S., Amey, M., and Chen, A. *Open to View: Practice and Purpose in General Education 1988: A Final Report to the Exxon Education Foundation.* University Park: Pennsylvania State University Center for the Study of Higher Education, 1989.

Toombs, W., and Tierney, W. G. *Meeting the Mandate: Renewing the College and Departmental Curriculum.* Washington, D.C.: George Washington University, 1991.

Trowler, P., and Knight, P. "Organizational Socialization and Induction in Universities: Reconceptualizing Theory and Practice." *Higher Education,* 1999, *37*(2), 177–195.

Tyler, R. *Basic Principles of Curriculum Development.* Chicago: University of Chicago Press, 1950.

van Vught, F. A. "Intrinsic and Extrinsic Aspects of Quality Assessment in Higher Education." In D. F. Westerheijden, J. Brennan, and P.A.M. Maassen (eds.), *Changing Contexts of Quality Assessment.* Utrecht: Lemma, 1994.

Werner, C. M., and Baxter, L. "Temporal Qualities of Relationships: Organismic, Transactional and Dialectical Views." In M. L. Knapp and G. R. Miller (eds.), *Handbook of Interpersonal Communications.* (2nd ed.) Thousand Oaks, Calif.: Sage, 1994.

JAMES L. RATCLIFF is president and senior consultant, Performance Associates Postsecondary Consulting, Pueblo West, Colorado.

INDEX

AAC&U. *See* Association of American Colleges and Universities (AAC&U)
Academic planning, 101–103
Accrediting associations, 22–23
Accrediting Board for Engineering Technology, 22
Active learning, 57, 59
Advanced courses, 14
Advising council, 48, 64
Advising students, 60, 73
AIS. *See* Guaranteed associate of integrated studies (AIS) degree
Alfred, R. L., 57, 59
Altman, I., 105, 107, 110
American Association of Community and Junior Colleges, 57, 59
American Pluralism and the College Curriculum (Association of American Colleges and Universities), 99
American University: barriers to change at, 43–44; coherence at, 93–94; course clustering at, 48–49; course review at, 48–49; criticisms of, 47; curricular areas at, 40–41; faculty development at, 44–46; faculty's response to change at, 43, 44; faculty's role at, 41; financial issues at, 44–45; future of, 49; goals of, 41–42; impact of change at, 42–43; innovation at, 44–45; origins of general education at, 39–40; overview of, 4; planning model of, 101–102; program evaluation at, 43–44, 46–48; quality of teaching at, 45–46; recommended changes at, 47–48; student demographics at, 39; students' response to change at, 44; technology use at, 45–46
Amey, M., 1, 3, 9, 14, 15, 17, 19, 21, 26, 27n.1
Angelo, T. A., 57
Applebee, A. N., 103
Aristotle, 109
Assessment: at Cascadia Community College, 61, 66–67; of GEFAP assistants, 45; importance of, 17; prevalence of, 13; role of, in change process,

17–18, 19; of student learning, 17–18, 19; of students upon entering college, 106; of writing assignments, 78. *See also* Program evaluation
Associate faculty, 66
Associate of integrated studies degree. *See* Guaranteed associate of integrated studies (AIS) degree
Associated New American Colleges, 76
Association of American Colleges, 85, 86, 87, 98, 105
Association of American Colleges and Universities (AAC&U), 2, 7, 9, 31, 76, 99
Association of Governing Boards of Universities and Colleges, 57
Astin, A., 57, 58–59, 59

B.A. degree, 14–15
Baccalaureate institutions, 10–11, 14
Bakhtin, M. M., 111
Banta, T. W., 17
Barnett, R., 104
Barr, R., 57, 59
Basic skills, 55, 56
Baxter, L. A., 105, 106, 107, 109, 110, 111, 112, 113
Bennett, W. J., 89, 98
Berkenkotter, C., 111
Best practices, 62
Blackboard site, 46
Blackburn, R. T., 1
Bloom, A., 98
Bok, D., 57
Bowen, R. C., 59
Boyer, E., 36, 89, 98
Brown, B. B., 105, 107, 110
B.S. degree, 14–15
Buckley, S., 33
Bush Foundation, 78–80

CAO 2000 survey, 2, 9–10, 86
CAO 2002 survey, 89
Capstone course, 7, 34, 90
Career opportunities, 42, 55–56, 79, 92
Carter, P., 57, 59

Distribution requirements, 13, 90, 107
Diversity issues: at Hamline University, 80–81; review of, 16
Doctoral institutions, 10–11, 14
Dolence, M. G., 55, 56, 58, 59
Dressel, P. L., 1
D'Souza, D., 99
Dusenbery, V. A., 77

e-Academics, 45–46
Efficient causation, 109
Electronic portfolios, 64
Elton, L., 107, 115
Employee Learning Institute, 5, 65
Engaging Cultural Legacies program, 31
Evergreen State College, 64
Expectations, 57
Experiential learning, 14, 49
External oppositions, 113–114

Faculty: needs of, 25–26; response to change at American University, 43, 44; rewards for, 77–78; role at American University, 41; role at Cascadia Community College, 59; role in Hamline Plan, 71, 73; support for, 66
Faculty committees, 2
Faculty demographics, at Franklin Pierce College, 30
Faculty development: at American University, 44–46; for Hamline Plan, 73–74, 76, 77
Faculty-student interaction, 59
Fairweather, J. S., 1, 3, 9, 14, 15, 17, 21, 26, 27n.1
Ferren, A. R., 40
50 Hours (Cheney, L.), 98
Financial issues: at American University, 44–45; at Franklin Pierce College, 30–31; at Hamline University, 78–80
Fit for purpose, 101
Ford Foundation, 77
Foreign language courses, 20
Formal causation, 109
Fragmentation. See Coherence
Franklin Pierce College: barriers to change at, 30–31; concerns of, 32–33, 36; curriculum overview of, 32–35; development of new curricular plan at, 31–35; faculty demographics at, 30; financial issues at, 30–31; goals of, 33–35; overview of, 3, 29–30; program evaluation at, 35

Freiberg, J., 55
Freiberg, K., 55
Freshman seminars, 14, 16, 72–74, 81–82
Front-line teaching, 41
Fuhrmann, B. S., 104
Functional changes, 102, 103
Functional opposite, 106, 107

Gaff, J. G., 1, 2, 3, 8, 9, 10, 14, 15, 17, 21, 24, 27n.1, 69, 74, 87, 97, 105, 107, 112
Gaffney, M. A., 22
Games, 58–59
Gamson, Z., 57, 59, 90
Garcia, M., 22
Garland, M., 55
Gates, B., 57, 58
Gates, S. M., 15
GE 2000 survey, 2, 9–10, 86
GEFAP. See General Education Faculty Assistance Program (GEFAP)
General College at the University of Minnesota, 1
General Education Committee, 40, 41, 46, 48, 71
General education curriculum: characteristics of, 12–13; course requirements in, 19–21, 27n.2; criticisms of, 86; current state of, 115–116; definition of, 1; governance of, 2; importance of, 69; organization of, 21–22; origin of, 1; overview of, 1–2; past studies of, 1; as priority, 10; problem of, 4; reported innovations in, 13–14; review of, 15–16
General Education Faculty Assistance Program (GEFAP), 44–46
George Mason University, 102
Gilbert, S. W., 58
Global studies, 20–21, 41, 77
GOALI project (Grant Opportunities for Academic Liaisons with Industry), 79
Goals: at American University, 41–42; and assessment of student learning, 18, 19; of Cascadia Community College, 56–57; clarity of, 13; and coherence, 89, 94; definition of, 94; of Franklin Pierce College, 33–35; of freshman seminars, 72; link between course requirements and, 13
Gollattscheck, J. F., 59
Graff, G., 88
Grasha, A. F., 104

Middle States Association of Colleges and Schools, 1, 4, 22, 23, 46
Minority students, 54, 80–81
Mission: of Cascadia Community College, 52, 59–61; of Hamline University, 71, 75; importance of, 12
Modeling, 83
Molecular biotechnology course, 76
Montgomery, B. M., 105, 106, 107, 109, 110, 111, 112, 113
Motivation, 58

National Endowment for the Humanities, 31
National Institute of Education, 98
National Science Foundation, 78–79
Natural science courses, 20, 41
NEASC. See Northeastern Association of Schools and Colleges (NEASC)
NEASC Standard 4—Programs and Instruction, 33
Neave, G., 97, 100
New England Association of Schools and Colleges, 3, 23, 32
A New Vitality in General Education (Association of American Colleges), 87, 105
Newmann, F. M., 57, 58
Newton, R. R., 86, 87, 110
Nichols, J., 31
Norman, D., 57, 58, 59
Norris, D. M., 56, 58, 59
North Central Association for Colleges and Schools, 23
Northeastern Association of Schools and Colleges (NEASC), 33
Northwest Association of Schools, Colleges and Universities, 4, 23, 53

O'Banion, T., 57, 59
Oregon State University, 64
The Outcomes Primer: Reconstructing the College Curriculum (Stiehl, R. & Lewchuk, L.), 54

Paired courses, 14
Palomba, C. A., 17
Part-time faculty, 66
Pascarella, E. T., 57, 59, 111
Perfection, 101
Philosophy courses, 20
Physical education courses, 20
Pierce Plan. See Franklin Pierce College

Pierce Plan Committee, 31
Pirsig, R., 100, 113
Policy on Inter-College Transfer and Articulation, 53
Portfolios, 60, 64
Portland State University, 99
Poster sessions, 82
Practical liberal arts, 70–71, 72, 91–92
Praxis, 111
Preparing Future Faculty program, 76
Private institutions, 53
Program evaluation: at American University, 43–44, 46–48; emergence of, 100; at Franklin Pierce College, 35; importance of, 15; role of, in change process, 15–16. See also Assessment
Program improvement. See Change
Program quality, 100–101, 103–105
Program updates, 26
Project-based learning, 55
Purpose, fit for, 101

Quality, program, 100–101, 103–105
Queens College, 31

Ramaley, J., 99
Ratcliff, J. L., 1, 2, 6, 7, 8, 9, 10, 22, 25, 85, 87, 88, 90, 91, 93, 97, 103, 104, 105, 106, 107, 108, 111, 115
Reardon, M., 99
Reed, C., 31
Reform. See Change
Reification, 111–112
Relational dialectics, 105
Remedial courses, 14
Research institutions, 10–11, 14
Retention, 26
Richart, V., 4, 51, 54, 106
Ritkin, J., 55, 59
Robinson, S., 54
Rowley, D. J., 55
Rudolph, F., 100–101
Rychlak, J. F., 109

Scheduling constraints, 91
Schneider, C. G., 7
Secretary's Commission on Achieving Necessary Skills (SCANS), 55–56
Seminars, 14, 16, 63, 72–74, 81–82
Senge, P., 93
Senior thesis, 14
Service-learning experiences, 14

Back Issue/Subscription Order Form

Copy or detach and send to:
Jossey-Bass, A Wiley Imprint, 989 Market Street, San Francisco CA 94103-1741

Call or fax toll-free: Phone 888-378-2537 6:30AM – 3PM PST; Fax 888-481-2665

Back Issues: Please send me the following issues at $29 each
(Important: please include series initials and issue number, such as HE114.)

_____

_____

_____

$ _____   Total for single issues

$ _____   SHIPPING CHARGES: SURFACE   Domestic   Canadian
                                               First Item $5.00 $6.00
                                               Each Add'l Item $3.00 $1.50
                  For next-day and second-day delivery rates, call the number listed above.

Subscriptions: Please __start __renew my subscription to *New Directions for Higher Education* for the year 2____at the following rate:

U.S.	__Individual $80	__Institutional $160
Canada	__Individual $80	__Institutional $200
All Others	__Individual $104	__Institutional $234
Online Subscription		__Institutional $176

**For more information about online subscriptions visit
www.interscience.wiley.com**

$ _____   Total single issues and subscriptions (Add appropriate sales tax for your state for single issue orders. No sales tax for U.S. subscriptions. Canadian residents, add GST for subscriptions and single issues.)

__Payment enclosed (U.S. check or money order only)
__VISA __MC __AmEx # _____ Exp. Date _____
Signature _____ Day Phone _____
__ Bill Me (U.S. institutional orders only. Purchase order required.)

Purchase order # _____
                 Federal Tax ID13559302   GST 89102 8052

Name _____

Address _____

_____

Phone _____ E-mail _____

For more information about Jossey-Bass, visit our Web site at www.josseybass.com

HE120 Leveraging Resources Through Partnerships
Lawrence G. Dotolo, John B. Noftsinger, Jr.
Provides examples of the benefits of consortial and external partnerships
that have proven to be successful for all the participants. Covers such topics
as leveraging resources, K–12 partnerships, economic development,
community development, workforce development, technology partnerships,
library cooperation, partnerships to serve the military, group purchasing,
inter-institutional faculty collaboration, television partnerships, cooperation
in international programs, and assessing a consortium's effectiveness.
ISBN: 0-7879-6333-X

HE119 Building Robust Learning Environment in Undergraduate Science,
Technology, Engineering, and Mathematics
Jeanne Narum
Acknowledging the growing national need for a well-equipped talent pool
from which the scientific, technical, and engineering workforce in the
twenty-first century will be drawn, this volume examines ways that trustees,
presidents, provosts, and deans can commit to national objectives and
translate them into action at the local level. It challenges academic leaders
to take immediate and informed action to guarantee undergraduate access to
programs of the highest quality that prepare them for life and work in the
world beyond the campus.
ISBN: 0-7879-6332-1

HE118 Using Benchmarking to Inform Practice in Higher Education
Barbara E. Bender, John H. Schuh
This volume provides different perspectives on the application of
benchmarking in higher education. Authors present conceptual overviews
and organizational examples of how benchmarking can be used in colleges
and universities. The reader will develop an appreciation of benchmarking as
an administrative tool, including a greater awareness of its strengths and
limitations. Administrators or faculty members in higher education will be
able to develop their own strategies for using benchmarking in their practice.
ISBN: 0-7879-6331-3

HE117 Internationalizing Higher Education
Beth H. Carmical and Bruce W. Speck
This volume provides insights into how administrators, professors, and
students can promote the internationalizing effort. Thus, chapters are
devoted to promoting the effort by explaining how to help students from
other countries be successful in the U.S. classroom, how to provide
opportunities for native students and professors to work and study overseas,
how to develop exchange programs, and how to help nonnative families
adjust to U.S. culture. For those interested in how to internationalize higher
education, this volume provides a wealth of practical advice.
ISBN: 0-7879-6290-2

HE116 Understanding the Role of Academic and Student Affairs Collaboration in
Creating a Successful Learning Environment
Adrianna Kezar, Deborah J. Hirsh, Cathy Burack
Presents authentic models of collaboration that will help to develop
successful student leaders for the next century. Argues that educators must
show students by their own behavior that they believe in the power of
collaboration, while still acknowledging that partnerships can be messy and

frustrating. The topic of collaboration between academic and student affairs is now more important than ever if colleges and universities are to educate students for the new collaborative environment.
ISBN: 0-7879-5784-4

HE115   Technology Leadership: Communication and Information Systems in Higher Education
George R. Maughan
Decisions about investments in information system infrastructure are among the most important—and costly—decisions campus and system administrators make. A wide variety of needs must be accommodated: those of students, faculty, and administrators themselves. This volume will help mainstream administrators think through the decision making process.
ISBN: 0-7879-5783-6

HE114   Developing and Implementing Service-Learning Programs
Mark Canada, Bruce W. Speck
Examines service learning—education that brings together students, teachers, and community partners in ways that foster the student's responsible citizenship and promotes a lifelong involvement in civic and social issues.
ISBN: 0-7879-5782-8

HE113   How Accreditation Influences Assessment
James L. Ratcliff, Edward S. Lubinescu, Maureen A. Gaffney
Examples of working programs include new methods of distance-education program assessment, an institutional accreditation self-study at the University of Vermont, and the Urban Universities Portfolio Project.
ISBN: 0-7879-5436-5

HE112   Understanding the Role of Public Policy Centers and Institutes in Fostering University-Government Partnerships
Lynn H. Leverty, David R. Colburn
Examines innovative approaches to developing the structure of programs in both traditional academic environments and in applied research and training; attracting and rewarding faculty engaged in public service; and determining which policy issues to approach at institutional levels.
ISBN: 0-7879-5556-6

HE111   Understanding the Work and Career Paths of Midlevel Administrators
Linda K. Johnsrud, Vicki J. Rosser
Provides information to help institutions develop recruitment efforts to fill midlevel administration positions and enlighten individuals about career possibilities in midlevel administration.
ISBN: 0-7879-5435-7

HE110   Moving Beyond the Gap Between Research and Practice in Higher Education
Adrianna Kezar, Peter Eckel
Provides suggestions for overcoming the research-practice dichotomy, such as creating a learning community that involves all the stakeholders, and using campus reading groups to help practitioners engage with scholarship.
ISBN: 0-7879-5434-9

HE109   Involving Commuter Students in Learning
        Barbara Jacoby
        Provides ways to create communities that meet the needs of students who
        live off-campus—from building a sense of community within individual
        courses to the creative use of physical space, information technology, living-
        learning communities, and experiential education programs.
        ISBN: 0-7879-5340-7

HE108   Promising Practices in Recruitment, Remediation, and Retention
        Gerald H. Gaither
        Identifies the best practices for recruitment, remediation, and retention,
        describing lessons learned from innovative and successful programs across
        the nation, and shows how to adapt these efforts to today's diverse
        populations and technological possibilities.
        ISBN: 0-7879-4860-8

HE107   Roles and Responsibilities of the Chief Financial Officer
        Lucie Lapovsky, Mary P. McKeoan-Moak
        Offers strategies for balancing the operating and capital budgets,
        maximizing net enrollment revenues, containing costs, planning for the
        resource needs of technology, identifying and managing risks, and
        investing the endowment wisely.
        ISBN: 0-7879-4859-4

HE106   Best Practices in Higher Education Consortia: How Institutions Can Work
        Together
        Lawrence G. Dotolo, Jean T. Strandness
        Gives detailed accounts of activities and programs that existing consortia have
        already refined, providing practical models that can be replicated or modified
        by other institutions, and describes how to start and sustain a consortium.
        ISBN: 0-7879-4858-6

HE105   Reconceptualizing the Collegiate Ideal
        J. Douglas Toma, Adrianna J. Kezar
        Explores how administration, student affairs, and faculty can work together
        to redefine the collegiate ideal, incorporating the developmental needs of a
        diverse student body and the changes in higher education's delivery and
        purpose.
        ISBN: 0-7879-4857-8

HE104   The Growing Use of Part-Time Faculty: Understanding the Causes
        and Effects
        David W. Leslie
        Presents analyses of the changes in academic work, in faculty careers, and in
        the economic conditions in higher education that are associated with the
        shift away from full-time academic jobs. Issues for research, policy, and
        practices are also discussed.
        ISBN: 0-7879-4249-9

HE103   Enhancing Productivity: Administrative, Instructional, and Technological
         Strategies
         James E. Groccia, Judith E. Miller
         Presents a multi-faceted approach for enhancing productivity that
         emphasizes both cost-effectiveness and the importance of bringing together
         all segments of the educational economy—institutions, faculty, students, and
         society—to achieve long-term productivity gains.
         ISBN: 0-7879-4248-0

HE102   Minority-Serving Institutions: Distinct Purposes, Common Goals
         Jamie P. Merisotis, Colleen T. O'Brien
         Serves as a primer on the growing group of minority-serving institutions,
         with the goal of educating leaders at mainstream institutions, analysts, and
         those at minority-serving institutions themselves about their distinct
         purposes and common goals.
         ISBN: 0-7879-4246-4

HE101   The Experience of Being in Graduate School: An Exploration
         Melissa S. Anderson
         Addresses the graduate experience from the standpoint of the students
         themselves. Presents what students have reported about their experience
         through interviews, surveys, ongoing discussions, and autobiographies.
         ISBN: 0-7879-4247-2

HE99   Rethinking the Dissertation Process: Tackling Personal and Institutional
         Obstacles
         Lester F. Goodchild, Kathy E. Green, Elinor L. Katz, Raymond C. Kluever
         Identifies the institutional patterns and support structures that enhance the
         dissertation process, and describes how the introduction of dissertation-
         stage financial support and workshops can quicken completion rates.
         ISBN: 0-7879-9889-3

HE98   The Professional School Dean: Meeting the Leadership Challenges
         Michael J. Austin, Frederick L. Ahearn, Richard A. English
         Focuses on the demanding leadership roles assumed by deans of social work,
         law, engineering, nursing, and divinity, providing case illustrations that
         illuminate the deanship experience at other professional schools.
         ISBN: 0-7879-9849-4

HE97   The University's Role in Economic Development: From Research to Outreach
         James P. Pappas
         Offers models the academy can use to foster the ability to harness the
         research and educational resources of higher education institutions as well
         as the potential of state and land-grant universities to provide direct services
         for local and regional economic development through outreach missions.
         ISBN: 0-7879-9890-7

NEW DIRECTIONS FOR HIGHER EDUCATION
IS NOW AVAILABLE ONLINE AT WILEY INTERSCIENCE

What is Wiley InterScience?

Wiley InterScience is the dynamic online content service from John Wiley & Sons delivering the full text of over 300 leading scientific, technical, medical, and professional journals, plus major reference works, the acclaimed *Current Protocols* laboratory manuals, and even the full text of select Wiley print books online.

What are some special features of Wiley InterScience?

Wiley InterScience Alerts is a service that delivers table of contents via e-mail for any journal available on Wiley InterScience as soon as a new issue is published online.

Early View is Wiley's exclusive service presenting individual articles online as soon as they are ready, even before the release of the compiled print issue. These articles are complete, peer-reviewed, and citable.

CrossRef is the innovative multi-publisher reference linking system enabling readers to move seamlessly from a reference in a journal article to the cited publication, typically located on a different server and published by a different publisher.

How can I access Wiley InterScience?

Visit http://www.interscience.wiley.com

Guest Users can browse Wiley InterScience for unrestricted access to journal Tables of Contents and Article Abstracts, or use the powerful search engine.

Registered Users are provided with a *Personal Home Page* to store and manage customized alerts, searches, and links to favorite journals and articles. Additionally, Registered Users can view free Online Sample Issues and preview selected material from major reference works.

Licensed Customers are entitled to access full-text journal articles in PDF, with select journals also offering full-text HTML.

How do I become an Authorized User?

Authorized Users are individuals authorized by a paying Customer to have access to the journals in Wiley InterScience. For example, a university that subscribes to Wiley journals is considered to be the Customer. Faculty, staff and students authorized by the university to have access to those journals in Wiley InterScience are Authorized Users. Users should contact their Library for information on which Wiley journals they have access to in Wiley InterScience.

ASK YOUR INSTITUTION ABOUT WILEY INTERSCIENCE TODAY!